John Ruffini

The Paragreens

On a Visit to Paris

John Ruffini

The Paragreens
On a Visit to Paris

ISBN/EAN: 9783741174735

Manufactured in Europe, USA, Canada, Australia, Japa

Cover: Foto ©Andreas Hilbeck / pixelio.de

Manufactured and distributed by brebook publishing software (www.brebook.com)

John Ruffini

The Paragreens

COLLECTION
OF
BRITISH AUTHORS

TAUCHNITZ EDITION.

VOL. 1010.

THE PARAGREENS BY JOHN RUFFINI.

IN ONE VOLUME.

TAUCHNITZ EDITION.

By the same Author,

LAVINIA	2 vols.
DOCTOR ANTONIO	1 vol.
LORENZO BENONI	1 vol.
VINCENZO	2 vols.
A QUIET NOOK	1 vol.
CARLINO	1 vol.

THE PARAGREENS

ON A VISIT TO PARIS.

BY

JOHN RUFFINI

AUTHOR OF
"DOCTOR ANTONIO," "A QUIET NOOK," ETC.

COPYRIGHT EDITION.

LEIPZIG

BERNHARD TAUCHNITZ

1869.

CONTENTS.

		Page
CHAPTER I.	En Route	1
— II.	Bivouac	18
— III.	Début in Paris	36
— IV.	Hero-Worship	54
— V.	Short but Instructive	74
— VI.	The Exhibition	89
— VII.	More Treats	101
— VIII.	The Escapade	115
— IX.	Highly Confidential	136
— X.	Between the Cup and the Lip . .	146
— XI.	Mysterious	159
— XII.	At Corazza's	171
— XIII.	Jacques Bonhomme	187
— XIV.	Dinner in the Rue las Cases . .	204
— XV.	Catastrophe Number One . . .	225
— XVI.	Catastrophe Number Two . . .	236
— XVII.	Mrs. Paragreen to the Rescue . .	248

THE PARAGREENS.

CHAPTER I.

En Route.

"EMMA, square your elbows, my dear — stick out your arms, Arabella; see, this way — stand by Tobo; steady, boy, steady — Dora, you and Da, lay fast hold of the tails of my coat; — when the door opens, all of you keep as close to my heels as you can. I am going to have a try for a carriage to ourselves — once in, we'll call out 'Complet,' French for 'full,' remember, and trundle away to Paris as comfy, comfy as can be; eh, Mrs. Paragreen?"

The circumstances under which the foregoing directions were issued, in thrilling whispers, by Mr. Sylvester Paragreen, of Eden Villa, Peckham, to his wife and offspring, (four pledges of affection in different stages of promising progression,) made pardonable, nay justified, the excitement of the speaker; perhaps necessitated the plan of strategy so graphically imaged forth by word and gesture.

Suppose five hundred people caged within a space just large enough to hold a moiety of the number,— suppose, in the heart of each of these five hundred people, a frantic craving to be foremost, a frantic determination to be so by fair means or foul — and you may then easily picture to yourself the uproar and confusion exhibited in the waiting-room of the Boulogne Railway terminus, on this blessed 19th of August 1855. The swell in the channel, midway between the white cliffs of Albion and the opposite dusky French coast, was not half so terrific as the swell of human waves compressed within the narrow limits of those four walls. The company was almost exclusively English, and therefore most respectable,— of that, there could be no doubt. Perhaps the combined effects of a paroxysm of loyalty, (they were running after the Gracious Majesty of England, who had passed on to Paris the day before,) and the heat of the dogdays, might account for the extra activity of the bump of combativeness displayed on this occasion by these true-hearted subjects.

Could the philosopher who said that "man was a wolf to man" have been a spectator of the scene, how he would have relished the sight of this small section of society in a state of nature, (plus, the wearing apparel, minus, luckily, the tomahawk,) waging war on each other,—of ladies, with the sourest or sweetest of faces, battering alike people's legs, or poking at people's eyes, with their dangling bags, and parasols brandished aloft,—of gentlemen, with dubious or irreproachable linen, smelling of patchouly or a fresh dram, as the case might be, pushing madly forwards, as if for life's sake, and using their elbows cruelly as wedges,—of young and old, high and low, equally bent on escalading, or violently suppressing the living obstacle in their way, undeterred by expostulations, cries, groans, wailing of babies, threats, and—oh shame! something far worse.

And all this tear and wear, all this scrambling, squeezing, trampling, all this ferocious competition in its most coarse and ugly shape, what was it for? merely to obtain the place, and carry the position —judge if the defence of it was a trifle—occupied by Mr. Paragreen and his family, — that is, close to the door giving access to the platform, and against the glass panes of which, Mr. Paragreen and his two little daughters, Emma and Arabella, were at that moment flattening their noses.

But the Paragreens were equal to the emergency. Tobo, a stout lad of seventeen, with his mother and eldest sister, formed the rear-guard, and stood their ground bravely. Mrs. and Miss Paragreen had dropped their travelling bags on the ground, an impromptu palisade between themselves and their assailants. Altogether, the family, as it stood in a double row, three abreast, looked like a miniature Macedonian phalanx, and one in which it would be difficult to espy or force an entrance. The resemblance was the more perfect, that the four broad-brims, worn by the female Paragreens, — those delicious chocolate-complexioned straw hats, so immortalized by Punch, did not represent amiss the bucklers, under cover of which, that famous ancient corps used to march.

"Are you sure the luggage is safe?" suddenly asked Mrs. Paragreen.

The luggage was the lady's mania.

"Quite safe, my dear, I have got a ticket for it."

"Where?" inquired the lady anxiously.

"Why! in my waistcoat pocket, with our other tickets."

"Are you quite certain, now, Mr. Paragreen?—you had better look before it's too late."

"My dear, I am so jammed."

"Nonsense — give me that bag," making a snatch at it.

Mr. Paragreen put his hand into the right side pocket — "Bless my heart!" he ejaculated.

"I thought so!" groaned Mrs. Paragreen.

"Here they are!" proclaimed Mr. Paragreen, red as a furnace, flourishing a thin piece of paper, and six slips of card.

"I'll bet anything you'll lose them as you did when —" a great push from behind compromised for an instant the equilibrium of the speaker, and stopped the phrase.

"If that nasty fellow outside would only open the door!" grumbles Mr. Paragreen, who feels horridly hot — having, besides Emma and Arabella, three umbrellas, four parasols, a large bag, and a waterproof garment to take care of.

The nasty fellow outside does not choose to open the door, but continues calmly examining the nice crowd inside, with the expressive eye of an amateur of natural history, scrutinizing a collection of caged wild beasts; indeed, he hears yells from within which might lead any one to suppose that a menagerie was waiting for first-class places. The survey over, he takes a turn up and then a turn down, suddenly starts off on some unknown errand, as if going away for ever — dashes back like a thunderbolt — flings the door open — hastily withdraws, and seeks safety in flight.

The shout and rush that follow are tremendous — the earth quakes as if under the tread of ten thousand buffaloes. The Family keep their place at the head of the race, they do not run, they fly — the Derby's won. "All right!" sings out Mr. Paragreen, pouncing on a carriage, the door of which is half open. Tobo pushes in the ladies while his father defends the dearly-bought conquest against all invaders. "Now, papa!" cries Tobo from his seat. Papa jumps on the steps in high glee.

"Complet, Monsieur!" says a voice from the inside.

A bucket of cold water thrown over his head, streaming with perspiration, would have caused Mr. Paragreen a less disagreeable surprise than this politely-toned "complet," and the subsequent discovery that in the carriage he had fondly fancied all his own, were three unknown persons, a lady and two gentlemen. The one who had uttered the fatal sentence was an elderly military gentleman, with large grey moustaches and tuft, wearing a red rosette in his button-hole.

"Commong, complette, Monseer?" asks Mr. Paragreen pugnaciously.

"Comptez plutôt, Monsieur!" answers he of the red rosette, "un, deux, trois, quatre, cinq, six, sept, huit." There was no disputing the accuracy of the reckoning.

Is was hard to be thus ousted from a carriage which he had in a manner conquered in the sweat of his face, and wherein sat his wife, his only son, and his three daughters — facts which, in Mr. Paragreen's eyes, established as clear a right for him to a place therein also, as if there existed a law to that effect:—banished, too, at the bidding of an old grey whiskerando of a Frenchman, with his trumpery bit of red ribbon! (Mr. Paragreen's partisanship of the French Alliance did not extend to French individuals.) Mr. Paragreen felt sorely aggrieved, as men are apt to do when they find an unforeseen obstacle suddenly interposed between themselves and their wishes. He further considered it due to himself, as the head of a family, to remonstrate, gently but firmly, against this unjust separation.

"Monseer! ma femme — ma place" — and then he came to a full stop.

The formula was most comprehensive, no doubt, but rather obscure to only commonly gifted minds. Poor Mr. Paragreen! he had in all good faith given himself credit for being an excellent French scholar — had been ostentatious, even rather bullying about his French — and now not to have a word at command to throw at that grim old Gaul! The flutter of his feelings had bewildered his memory.

"Plait-il?" said the Frenchman, having waited with patience for another noun or verb to make clear the little Englishman's meaning.

Mr. Paragreen was going to try again, when "En voiture! en voiture!" shouted the railway officials on all sides — bang, bang, bang went the doors.

"Papa! papa! make haste — you'll be left behind!" screamed all his darlings in chorus.

"Que faites vous là, Monsieur?" cried a voice with authority in its tones, "allons, into vagon, on part!" and the half-distracted Mr. Paragreen was seized, carried off, hurry-scurried from end to end of the long train in search of a seat nowhere to be found, until at last he was fain to be thankful when he was literally hurled into a carriage, where he met with about as friendly a reception as a housebreaker would at his own Eden villa.

As her husband was thus ravished from her sight, Mrs. Paragreen started forward and thrust her head and shoulders out of the window, following the eccentric movements of the familiar little form with undisguised anxiety. When her upper portion reappeared in the carriage, she curtly announced to her children

"He's all safe!" and then proceeded to some strange manipulations of her stiff silk dress, by which she managed not to sit upon it, but on a white garment with a handsome bordering—technically called "slip," we believe. This done, she settled down into the gloomy majesty of a wife forcibly and unjustly bereaved of her wedded lord.

The tenants of the carriage in which Mr. Paragreen had found a timely refuge, were but three; but they had managed things so nicely, that not a square inch of spare room was visible. The front seats were occupied by two ladies in the full indulgence of that horizontal line so dear to fair English travellers; and the whole of the back seats was engrossed by a middle-aged Briton, hedged in on either side by a fabulous outwork of carpet-bags, work-bags, dressing-case-bags, leather hand-bags, books, baskets, cushions, shawls, cloaks, wrappers, &c. Where was Mr. Paragreen to sit? How was Mr. Paragreen to sit? He pushed aside some of the inconvenient conveniencies on which he had alighted, and burrowed down to a seat, too full of his own grievances to notice the signs of ill-will his proceedings excited in the owners

of the cloaks, cushions, &c. Mr. Paragreen was in
that state of exasperation which seeks an outlet; but
his tirades against the absurd bad management of
French railroads and the unfair treatment of the
English, who paid their money for their places as
well as other people, fell flat;—even his attempts to
catch a sympathetic glance were defeated. There
was an evident determination on the part of his
companions to ignore his presence, and look as though
he were not. Nothing remained for him but to fold
his arms, shut his eyes, and strive to scrape together
a sufficiency of French phrases to form a powerful
speech, which he intended to deliver, on the first
opportunity, to the person he considered the usurper
of his seat. After a good deal of hard mental work,
Mr. Paragreen owned to himself that it was a hopeless business:—exhausted by conflicting feelings, he
drew the blind across his own peculiar side-window,
put his head in the corner, and went to sleep.

Mr. Paragreen had achieved his fifty-fifth year
without having ever visited France, without, indeed,
even contemplating the possibility of doing so some
day. Not that Mr. Paragreen disliked France par-

ticularly, or that he lacked that dose of self-sufficiency, the main strength as well as main peculiarity of the English abroad; but that travelling did not form one of the items in his plan of life; just as, perhaps, fox-hunting or racing hold no place in that of yours or mine. Mr. Paragreen had had the luck to make money in the cork-trade, and the good sense to give up business in time to enjoy his fortune. He had once made a hit, a famous hit—the invention of that celebrated, universally known, and universally accepted machine, which cuts, rounds, and throws off a thousand bottle-corks in the space of a thousand seconds.

To enjoy his well-earned *otium cum dignitate*, Mr. Paragreen had shifted his quarters from the city to the suburban Tivoli of Peckham, and set up quite a stylish establishment at Eden Villa, with a man in livery, and a boy in buttons, a double-bodied phaeton, and great grey horse—armorial bearings on the phaeton, crest on the harness, a governess, and tip-top singing-masters for his daughters—in short, all the comforts and elegancies of genteel life. Not that Mr. Paragreen aimed at playing the fashionable, as hinted by more than one of his less fortunate brethren, who made great fun of the crest, with which he now invariably sealed all letters and notes — not he, "a self-made man, a plain, practical, unpretending chap, with no nonsense about him," as he loved to describe himself. But his wife did—and he liked to humour her—and why should not he? After all, she had as good a right to be fashionable as most people. She was a Joliffe of Hackney, and if her father was a retired drysalter, there had been an admiral in the family — so at least ran the tradition—and there was an actual *bonâ fide* living Alderman Joliffe, her first cousin, who might any day be Lord Mayor. Now, as one of that respectable stock of the Joliffes, Mrs. Paragreen had a name to support, and duties to perform. Such, for instance, as to have all letters and cards presented to her on the salver bought for that purpose, and the button-bespattered boy following at her heels with the prayer-book, when she went to church. It was this keen sense of what she owed to her country, to her sovereign, to herself, and her maiden name, that had made her feel the propriety of going to the Paris Exhibition, on the auspicious occasion of Her Majesty's visit to the French capital.

This was her sole motive, and not, as hinted by ill-natured people, the circumstance of her neighbour, Mrs. Jones of Creeper's Lodge, the wealthy widow of the Russian tallow-merchant, having made it known that she had written to secure apartments in the Hôtel Bristol, Place Vendôme. Mrs. Jones preferred waiting a week — she was sorry she could not be present at the Queen's entry into Paris, she wished it could have been otherwise — but really she could not venture on any other place than the Hôtel Bristol.

To return.—Mrs. Paragreen had a vague impression that something would be wanting to the satisfaction of Queen Victoria and her imperial host, if the representatives of two most loyal families, such as the Joliffes and the Paragreens, did not give evidence of their respect, by following in the wake of the Head of the State. Mr. Paragreen shrugged his shoulders at what he considered the amiable weakness of his handsome partner, but did not argue the point — one ought to humour one's wife, you know. He made but one condition — no men, no maid-servants; went to his banker, filled his purse — and here they were, *en route*.

"Montreuil Vert, cinq minutes d'arrêt," cried the railway guards. Mr. Paragreen bolted from his seat on to the platform, and was by the side of the forbidden carriage, looking as disconsolate as the Peri at the gate of Paradise, except when he tried to look fierce at his antagonist of the grizzly beard. He repeated the same manœuvre at Abbeville, Hangest, and Amiens, where there was to be a stop of twenty minutes.

"Je n'y tiens plus, I will not run the risk of having my dreams haunted by that rueful face," said in French the military-looking gentleman, and, raising the hand of the lady by his side most respectfully to his lips, with a cordial pressure to that of her fellow-traveller, he got out of the carriage, saying to Mr. Paragreen as he passed, "Ma place est à votre service, Monsieur."

Mr. Paragreen did not wait to have the invitation repeated, but jumped at once into the Frenchman's vacated seat. "Better late than never!" he exclaimed with a little sort of triumph. "I should like to know what right that old French snipe had to sit comfortably in a carriage, while we were being battered to pieces in the waiting-room; — precious unfair, for I am sure he wasn't there no more than these other people."

"It's a pity you didn't find that out sooner, and stand up for your right like a man; you can crow loud enough when there's no danger," was the bitter sweet remark of the lady of Eden Villa.

"Bless my heart, my dear," responded Mr. Paragreen, a little crest-fallen, "how *is* one to make one's self heard with those guards continually roaring 'En voiture!' and all that. In England, you know, I would have had the matter sifted to the bottom, I would, in spite of his great moustache, and red ribbon."

"I say, Pa — suppose he had called you out?" exclaimed Tobo; "he's a regular old brick, I can see; it wouldn't be easy to shut him up."

"I wish you wouldn't make use of such low slang, Tobo," said his father reproachfully; "I wish you would behave like a gentleman, sir."

This impressive address put an end to a conversation which had caused the French lady and gentleman to exchange many a look and almost imperceptible smile.

"Is this Paris?" asked Mrs. Paragreen some time after, suddenly waking out of a nap.

Mr. Paragreen, who, of course, did not know, turned to the strangers, and said most interrogatively — "Parisse?"

"Non, Monsieur, c'est Pontoise," replied the gentleman, in a courteous tone; "nous serons à Paris dans trois quarts d'heure."

"It isn't Paris," explained Mr. Paragreen to his wife, "it's a place called Trocadero."

Mrs. Paragreen nudged his elbow, and whispered, "Don't speak to those people, they are vulgar."

The French lady and gentleman exchanged another look and smile.

Was it the lady's plain travelling dress in excellent taste, the complete absence of bouffans, crinoline, and jewelry about her, or the kiss bestowed on her hand; or was it the husband's polite haste in picking up Mrs. Paragreen's smart handkerchief, which had impressed the lady of Eden Villa with a sense of their vulgarity? Who can tell? We know for our own part, that we were unmercifully cut dead all the way from Turin to Chambery, by an English couple, to one of whom we had had the ungentlemanly weakness to resign our rights in the coupé of the mail.

In spite of Mrs. Paragreen's ominous predictions as to delay or danger, the train reached Paris at the appointed hour, and the whole family repaired in good marching order to the Salle des Bagages.

CHAPTER II.

Bivouac.

It took some considerable time to collect the luggage of our party, which, exclusive of what they themselves carried, consisted of seven trunks, four carpet bags, and six bonnet boxes. When Mrs. Paragreen went to see with her own eyes that all was safe, most dreadfully excited she became at missing one of the trunks — the one with her own peculiar treasures. It was no sooner found than Mr. Paragreen suddenly recollected, to his consternation and his wife's uncontrollable anger, that, in his change of carriages at Amiens, he had forgotten the umbrellas, parasols, waterproof, &c., confided to his care. Leaving Tobo in charge of the ladies and trunks, the poor little man rushed back to the platform, and, more favoured by luck than wisdom, recovered his property. Returning to his anxious family, radiant with success, he found a couple of *octroi* men, whose suspicion had been aroused by the unprecedented number of trunks and boxes belonging to the same party, insisting on having at least one of them opened — an operation which proved long and difficult, as no one of the keys fitted. At last when porters presented themselves with their customary cry of "Commissionnaires pour les bagages!" Mrs. Paragreen catching the word protested she would have no commissionnaires, — even thrust her parasol at one of them. This horror of commissionnaires originated in a firm belief, instilled into her by a dear friend, a lady who had long resided in Paris, that commissionnaires were disreputable characters, — in short, go-betweens, whose sole business in life was to carry love-letters; and that never, under any pretext whatever, ought respectable persons to have recourse to them.

Fortunately this new difficulty was overcome by the intervention of the railway official with "Interpreter" embroidered on his cap, who, on being apprized by Mrs. Paragreen herself of the cause of her strange behaviour, said he would send some porters, who were not commissionnaires — and so said, so done.

But, by this time, the last omnibus for conveying travellers to Hotels had been gone more than half an hour, leaving no other alternative than to send for a couple of citadines, in which, after the family with their addenda of small packages, four trunks, and three carpet bags, had been placed, there still remained three of the trunks, six bonnet boxes, and a carpet bag to be disposed of; and a third citadine had to be procured. "All right!" said Mr. Paragreen, in a cheerful voice, after giving the address of the Hotel where he intended to stop, and the three vehicles set off, the bulk of the luggage in the first, Mr. and Mrs. Paragreen with Arabella in the second, Tobo, Miss Paragreen, and Emma in the third.

It was eight o'clock in the evening. Crowds of people were sauntering in the streets and on the Boulevards, glad to breathe the cool air of evening after the sultriness of the day — crowds of people sat enjoying their coffee and cigars in front of cafés — crowds of omnibuses, hackney coaches, cabs, and private equipages of every kind, crossed and recrossed in every direction. English, French, Sardinian, and Turkish flags, were streaming out from shops and balconies. Paris, in fact, was looking as lively, coquettish, and bewitching, as only Paris can look, when she chooses. But most of the witchery of the scene — keenly enjoyed, though, by the younger Paragreens — was lost for the nonce on their respectable parents, who sat with their heads out of opposite windows — one watching with anxiety the citadine in the van — the other, the citadine in the rear. In this attitude they reached the Hôtel de la Cigogne, Rue St. Honoré; — recommended by Mrs. Paragreen's cousin, Alderman Joliffe, who had spent some days there, and whose lips had pronounced the dictum of "a clean, respectable, reasonable house," so reverentially inscribed in Mr. Paragreen's notebook.

Mr. Paragreen being a practical man who left as little as possible to chance, alighted and said he would see the rooms with his own eyes, and settle with the landlord, before any of the others got out, or any of the boxes were touched. The head waiter of the Hôtel de la Cigogne, in shirt sleeves, white cravat, and red slippers, was sitting astride a chair, his face to its back, puffing away at a cigar. The advent of the three citadines did not occasion any change in his posture — he did not even wink, an ominous sign indeed to the initiated.

"Avez vous les appartemengs?" asked Mr. Paragreen, walking straight up to this composed personage.

"I am not shore," replied the gentleman of the shirt sleeves, languidly rising.

"Je viens de Mr. Joliffe, Alderman of Londres," continued Mr. Paragreen.

This emphatic announcement made no visible impression on Shirtsleeves, who shuffled his way to a sort of wooden cage in the court-yard, tapped at its window, exchanged some words with the person on the perch within, and received a key.

"Gis way, Sar," and up a stair he pattered.

"Premier étage, s'il vous plaize," said Mr. Paragreen benevolently.

"Fust flour he is full," replied Redslippers, who stuck as fast to his English as the retired cork-merchant to his French, continuing his ascent as long as there were stairs to allow of the proceeding. Here he ushered Mr. Paragreen into a tolerably-sized room with two beds, and within which was a light closet with one bed, — the furniture of both rooms scanty, and not over clean.

"Trop haut et trop petitte," observed Mr. Paragreen, — adding in an explanatory tone, "manque un lit pour douce."

"Pour douze!" cried the Frenchman, startled for the first time out of his phlegm and his English.

"Pour douce," affirmed Mr. Paragreen, putting out two fingers.

"Ah! I comprehend, pour deux — verry good — we put a matelas to the ground."

Mr. Paragreen hesitated a moment, and then asked, "Combien la prix?"

"Two guinées for night."

"Bless my heart!" exclaimed Mr. Paragreen, in his turn giving up his French in his amazement, "two guineas for such a hole!"

"It is to take or to leave," said Shirtsleeves calmly.

"Then I leave it, Sir," said Mr. Paragreen tartly, going down the many flights of stairs like an India rubber ball, and repeating to himself, "Bless my heart! two guineas for such a hole! — wish you joy of it, my man, wish you joy!"

"Well?" inquired Mrs. Paragreen.

"Impudent rascal!" said Mr. Paragreen. "Do you know what he asked? Only two guineas a night! Two guineas, Ma'am, (laughing irately,) for two dirty pigeon-holes at the very top of the house! — they would be dear at half-a-crown! Lucky that I am not one to buy a pig in a poke."

"Où allons nous?" asked the coachman.

"Chez l'Hôtel," replied Mr. Paragreen.

"Quel Hôtel?"

"Tous les Hôtels," answered Mr. Paragreen.

The Jehu, rather divining than understanding Mr. Paragreen's meaning, telegraphed to his two brethren, and they all moved on down the Rue St. Honoré, stopping at the first hotel they came to. Out went Mr. Paragreen with the same inquiries for "appartemengs." "Plein comme un œuf," was the answer, "try next door." He did try at the next house, and the next but one, and the next to that, and at all the hotels in Rue St. Honoré, and received the same answer everywhere. Not a hole to be had.

"Very odd," remarked Mr. Paragreen, beginning to look blank; "I don't understand it at all."

"And it's growing quite dark," said Mrs. Paragreen; "the best thing we can do is to go back to the Seegong."

"What? go back to that dirty humbug of a place? I would rather sleep in the street," replied her husband; "it's a man's own fault, if, with money in his pocket, and a tongue in his head, he does not manage to find a good lodging for the night in Paris."

Since his French dialogue with the head waiter of the Cigogne, Mr. Paragreen had recovered part of that confidence in his own French powers of speech, which had been somewhat diminished during his railway journey.

"Oh allons nous?" asked the coachman again.

"Partout!" was the laconic rejoinder.

Up Rue Castiglione, and Rue de la Paix, down Rue des Petits Champs, up Rue Vivienne, down Rue Neuve des Augustins, went the doleful caravan. In and out of the coach was Mr. Paragreen every two minutes, as if for a wager; — not a spare room, not a closet to be had for love or money; — very tantalizing, when every second house, he plainly saw, was a hotel. There really seemed to be a general conspiracy to exclude our family from the shelter of a roof. The Boulevard des Capucines, and the Boulevard des Italiens proved, if possible, more unfeeling than all the rest put together. The long Rue de Richelieu had but one answer to the eager and perpetual inquiry for apartments, — silent, often frowning shakes of the head. The waiters had manifestly no patience to spare.

As eleven o'clock struck at the clock of the Palais Royal, the three citadines came to a full stop in the Place du Palais Royal. Mr. Paragreen was worn out by exertion, and Mrs. Paragreen not in the best of humours.

"Les chevaux sont fatigués," said coachman No. 1.

"Oh! ah!" answers Mr. Paragreen.

"Hôtel de Seegong," cried Mrs. Paragreen, roused into taking the lead. The Hôtel de la Cigogne being near at hand, the coachman made no objection, and drove thither. Shirtsleeves, with his white cravat and red slippers, was sitting on the same chair, puffing away at a cigar as before, in a reverie that prevented his noticing the three citadines, or hearing the voice of Mr. Paragreen calling to him from the coach window. Mr. Paragreen had to drink the dregs of the cup of bitterness, and get once more out of the citadine, and go up to the unruffled waiter. "Je prends des appartemengs," he said.

"No apartments now," returned the smoker laconically.

"I mean the rooms you showed me two hours ago."

"Gone — taken," replied Shirtsleeves, sending forth a remarkable column of smoke through his nose.

"I will give two guineas and a half," urged the Englishman.

"Not for a oondred dousand pounds," pronounced the despot in red slippers.

The discomfited Mr. Paragreen had no choice but to return to the carriage, and report progress to Mrs. Paragreen, whose milk of human kindness was beginning to sour. She received the sad intelligence with a toss of the head, and an insinuation that, if he had had the *goodness* to listen to *her* when she had first proposed to come back to this hotel, ten to one but they might have had the rooms. "But no, it is always the same with you, you must have your own way, you must;—where the *jeuce* is the man going now?" This last burst of Mrs. Paragreen's eloquence was occasioned by the coachman driving off without having received any orders.

"Bless my heart! how should I know?" cried Mr. Paragreen, popping his head out of the window, and roaring "Cochère! cochère!"—but the cocher appealed to did not stop, until, followed by his companions, he had once more reached the coachstand in the Place du Palais Royal.

"Les chevaux sont éreintés, Monsieur," said the driver, appearing at the door of the citadine.

"Oui," replied Mr. Paragreen knowingly.

"Ils ne peuvent plus marcher," continued the coachman.

"Oh!" ejaculated Mr. Paragreen.

"Si c'était une toute petite course, je ne dis

pas, mais aller comme ça au hasard, donner la chasse aux hôtels —"

"Oui, oui," put in Mr. Paragreen, catching at a familiar word, "aller à l'hôtel."

The coachman gave it up in despair, and returned to the coachbox.

"What does he say?" asked Mrs. Paragreen.

"Why, they all speak so fast, I can't make it out."

"I am afraid you know very little French after all," observed Mrs. Paragreen.

Mr. Paragreen made no attempt to defend his French; he had given it up, renounced it, repented of it.

"That's half-past eleven, I declare," cried Mrs. Paragreen — "are we going to stop here all night, Mr. Paragreen?"

"The coachman is mending something about the harness, I think," was Mr. Paragreen's rather wild supposition.

"I'm sure he is doing no such thing," said Mrs. Paragreen, after a survey of the person in question.

"Cochère!" called Mr. Paragreen, "aller à l'hôtel."

The cocher came down from his seat again, and tried to persuade his helpless fare to send a commissionnaire to search for a night's lodging for them.

The obnoxious word was no sooner uttered, than Mrs. Paragreen, with the vivacity of a war-horse at sound of trumpet, pricked up her ears, and vehemently exclaimed, — "No, no, I say, no commissionaire, — do you hear?"

"Eh bien! alors restez là où vous êtes," grumbled the coachman, quite out of patience.

Apparently the three coachmen knew how to make up their minds to an unavoidable evil, for they busied themselves about their horses, got them hay and water, and then climbed back to their seats, adopting the posture of men resolved to sleep, let what would happen. Mr. Paragreen made two faint efforts to rouse the driver of his own citadine, but was vigorously repulsed, with an exhortation to go to sleep, or at all events to let other people sleep.

In the meantime the noise and hum of the busy city gradually hushed; one after the other the gay shops and brilliant cafés put out their gas lights, and put up their shutters, leaving fair play to the silver radiance of the moon, now shining down as complacently on the three benighted citadines, as if they had not contained six forlorn houseless wanderers from Peckham. In another ten minutes scarcely a footfall broke the deep silence of midnight. The reality of their situation — that is, the necessity of bivouacking where they were — did not dawn on the understanding of the parent Paragreens until the ominous signs of the state of the world just mentioned, had, so to say, made palpable to them the uselessness and folly of a further search after lodgings for that night.

Then it was that Mrs. Paragreen, as some sort of comfort, fell foul of her husband, who, by his stupid notion of being practical, as she said, had exposed to all the inclemencies and dangers of a night spent in the open street, an innocent family, of whom he was the natural protector; and who, but for his pigheadedness, would have been by this time comfortably in their beds — at least, they might have had a ceiling, and not a coach roof over their heads; any garret was better than a coach and a coachstand. All she hoped was that this disgraceful way of spending their first night in Paris might not get wind. It only wanted this to put them under that abominable Mrs. Jones's feet for life. The very idea was enough to make her swear never to go to Peckham again!

At this climax the little Emma and Arabella began to cry, because they were hungry; and when Mr. Paragreen, in an ungovernable terror lest he should lose his way, had procured some cakes at a providential stall, bivouacking also at a corner of the Rue St. Honoré; the children then complained of being thirsty, and had to be carried to the pump of the coachstand; that done, they began to whimper that they were sleepy, and that they could not sleep, because they were afraid. And poor Mr. Paragreen had to do and to bear everything, to cheer and coax the little ones, to try to joke and make Mrs. Paragreen smile, to wander from citadine to citadine, though foot-sore, in order to satisfy himself that neither the one with Tobo and Ida — both fast asleep — nor the other with the luggage, was giving him the slip. And if by accident he sat quiet for five minutes, and his eyes involuntarily closed, he had immediately a nightmare of grizzly moustaches, red rosette, and "complets." Poor Mr. Paragreen counted every hour of that interminable night, and considered himself the most unhappy of living mortals; — little suspecting that hundreds and hundreds of his fellow-countrymen, and fellow-creatures — as was really the case — were faring at that identical moment as badly as himself, and even worse — encumbering the terminus of the various railroads, and lodging on the cold ground; though perhaps to lie down in any way would have proved a relief to our harassed hero.

At five in the morning, the coachmen having recovered their briskness and good-humour, the cavalcade was again set in motion, and the search renewed, and, after another two hours' perambulation, they had the good luck to reach the door of an hotel in the vicinity of the Madeleine, as an English family were taking their departure. This time Mr. Paragreen struck a bargain without insisting on a previous view of the vacated rooms; they proved to be high up, small, neither over clean nor over airy, but Mr. Paragreen was cured of his squeamishness.

He lauded the situation for being fashionable, but made no mention of an advantage, which, perhaps, in the present state of affairs, had greater weight with him, — viz., that the landlord and waiters all spoke English, and that the majority of the persons staying in the house were English also.

After the luggage had been carried up to their apartments (three small rooms), came the settling with the coachmen for the use of their citadines during eleven hours — twenty-one francs multiplied by three, gave the amount of sixty-three francs, not including drink-money. Mr. Paragreen paid the money without the least demur, but in spite of the assurances of landlord and waiters, looked on the transaction as a downright robbery, and in this belief will go to his grave. Thus practical Mr. Paragreen, who would not give fifty francs to sleep in a garret, paid sixty-three francs for a bivouac in the street.

The family were one and all worn out; so, after a substantial breakfast eaten in their own rooms, they adjourned to bed, where we leave them, wishing them pleasant dreams.

CHAPTER III.

Début in Paris.

REINVIGORATED by twenty hours of sound sleep, with only the casual interruption of a tea as solid as the morning's meal had been, the Paragreens rose upon the following day like giants refreshed, breakfasted, made themselves smart, and then sallied forth, phalanx-like, under cover of the famous round hats. As they hop their way, three abreast, down Rue Royale, and Rue Faubourg St. Honoré, bent on a visit to the Palais de l'Industrie, (we use the verb 'hop' advisedly, in our wish to figure forth as accurately as possible the peculiar gait of the family — a hop and a stride,) it may be as well to say a word of their personal appearance.

Little, active, and supple, Mr. Paragreen, though in reality born with the century, looks as if he had come into the world at least twenty years later. His step is so elastic you might suppose his legs to be made of some of his own best cork — his head vibrates from right to left, and left to right, like a mandarin's in a tea-shop — he frequently comes to a dead halt, peeps through a glass, pendant from his neck by a black ribbon, surveys people and things with an eye of speculation, and freely dispenses patronising smiles. If outward signs are to be trusted, we may set him down as an honest, good-natured, self-satisfied, rather pompous busybody. Dressed from head to foot in a yellow-greenish stuff, and with the most diminutive and flattest of green hats, Mr. Paragreen forcibly suggests the idea of a lizard out for an airing.

Mrs. Theodora Paragreen, commonly called by her husband "Dora," is a majestic woman of fifty, a head taller than her husband, and would be really a handsome creature but for her nose — a nose which her nearest and dearest cannot idealize — a nose that is a decided snub — a diminutive, undignified snub. Mrs. Paragreen dresses showily, wears plenty of crinoline, massive gold bracelets, (a serpent and a chain both of natural size,) and a profusion of costly gew-gaws. In this display of finery, combined with a certain toss of the head, in which she indulges occasionally, you read the bad taste and pride of a parvenu; in the quick glance and resolute carriage, a hasty temper, and a good deal of determination.

Ida, Miss Paragreen, styled Da, is the flattered portrait of her mother, (crinoline included,) with the addition of a well-shaped nose, and the subtraction of thirty years. She has large blue eyes, rich auburn hair, and that beautiful complexion found nowhere in such perfection as among healthy English girls. The only fault to be found with her is her foot, which, no doubt, is rather large; but who cares about a handsome girl's feet, particularly when fashion favours long dresses? A gentle, happy disposition is all that is legible on that smooth surface.

Tom, alias Tobo, is a tall, strong lad of seventeen, with open, turn-down shirt collars, blue jacket, cap to match, and half boots, into the perversely protruding high backs of which his trowsers as perversely stick themselves. He looks like an embryo Horse Guardsman, gives himself the airs of a man, and "won't be bullied."

We leave undescribed the small fry, Emma and
Arabella, eight and nine years of age; they have a
general resemblance to bantam chickens with be-
frilled little legs.

Mr. Paragreen had his own reasons for choosing
to go to the Exhibition by the Rue du Faubourg St.
Honoré, instead of proceeding thither by the Rue
Royale, Place de la Concorde, and the Champs
Elysées. Mr. Paragreen was a practical man, and
had resolved to kill two birds with one stone; to
speak without metaphor, Mr. Paragreen had in his
waistcoat pocket two cards — the large conjugal card
with —

"Mr. and Mrs. Paragreen,"
"Miss Paragreen, Eden Villa, Peckham,"

engraved in fine clear characters by Strongi'tharm;
and in very minute letters, by Mr. Paragreen himself, "Hôtel de l'Unicorne, Paris," — and his son
and heir's bachelor card with "Mr. Thomas Paragreen;" both of which he meant to leave, and ac-
tually did leave at the English Embassy in the Rue
du Faubourg St. Honoré.

"Nobody can accuse me of being a tuft-hunter,

thank God," said our little friend, stepping back lightly through the porte-cochère; "every one knows I am a self-made man; but I respect my country, and I look upon it as an Englishman's duty to shew that he upholds the representative of that country in a foreign land."

"Will the 'Bassador ask us to his house?" inquired Tobo.

"The Ambassador, sir," replied Mr. Paragreen, with grave emphasis, "may invite us on account of our being English and his fellow-subjects, to partake of some of the festivities given in honour of our most gracious Queen, — it is impossible for me to say whether he will or not. We must not set our hearts, however, on such vain distinctions, but look for — for honest recreation and — and — all that, you know, within ourselves."

"People make such a fuss about Paris," said Mrs. Paragreen in a disturbed voice, "I am sure I see nothing so wonderful about the streets; for my part, I think the Edgeware Road beats this hollow."

"It's in the public monuments, my dear, that Paris tops us," returned Mr. Paragreen, fixing his glass to his eye, "monuments like this 'Elysée Impérial;'" and he brought the whole party to a standstill, — "the residence of his Imperial Majesty, Napoleon III."

"Can't you call a building a building, Mr. Paragreen, and not talk of it as if it were a tombstone?" was the lady's interruption, while Tobo exclaimed, "Lor, Pa, I always thought young Nap put up at the sign of the Tuileries."

Before Mr. Paragreen could reply to his wife, or reprove his irreverent son, Mrs. Paragreen started violently, and pinching his arm, almost screamed aloud, "Good gracious me! — look, what a number of Turks!" and she pointed to the Zouaves, many of whom issued at that instant from the guard-room of the Palace.

"Ha! indeed! probably a Turkish regiment being formed in Paris, like our foreign legion, you know, somewhere or other near Folkstone. Great compliment the Emperor pays in having them about his person, — excellent taste, I call it, to have his allies to guard his own palace, eh!"

Thus conversing, they reached the Place Beauveau, and were about to enter the Avenue Marigny, leading into the Champs Elysées, when a carriage and four, preceded and followed by out-riders, emerged at a gentle trot from the Rue Miromenil, and went up the Rue du Faubourg, in the direction of the Barrière du Roule.

"The Emperor!" screamed Mrs. Paragreen, and away the family rushed in hot chase. But run as fast as they could, they could not manage to keep up with the four horses, now going at a brisk pace. "I saw the back of his head," cried Tobo, returning to his panting mother and sisters, mopping his face, which streamed with perspiration. "No; did you now, Tobo?" exclaimed both the little girls ready to cry, and with faces flushed and swelled by the heat.

"Never mind, my dears," said Mr. Paragreen, "we shan't want for opportunities of seeing the Imperial family, though, now I think of it, I am sure it could not be the Emperor, because, in Paris, they always beat the drum as he passes. But you must let me look about me," added Mr. Paragreen, stopping short, and casting his eyes around — "it strikes me that, if we take to the left, it will bring us direct to the Champs Elysées and the Exhibition."

"I wish you would buy a map of Paris at once, Sylvester," said Mrs. Paragreen, "then we should be sure of what we are about."

"I have got a capital map here, my dear," returned Sylvester, tapping his forehead, where the organ of locality is situated — "no dog ever had a better nose for game than I have for places—Didn't I tell you so?" he continued with a swagger, as they came to the Rond Point in the Champs Elysées, opposite the Avenue Montaigne, at the entrance of which were two Venetian masts, with streamers bearing the words, "Exposition des Beaux Arts."

"There it is," said Mr. Paragreen, pointing to the inscription. Mr. Paragreen's notions about the Exhibition were rather misty, and of such nice distinctions as an Exhibition of Industry, and one of the Fine Arts, he was entirely ignorant. With unquestioning confidence he led the way into the Avenue Montaigne, looking first to one side, then to the other, his glass a fixture to his eye, until he descried a long wooden building with a yellow

painted façade, whereon figured in large letters —
"Succursale de l'Exposition Universelle." The word
"Succursale" was not in our friend's vocabulary, but
"salle" was, and what could "Succursale" mean,
but a salle with a handle to its name?

"Here we are all right," cried Mr. Paragreen,
stiffening himself; "now what would have been the
use of a valet de place or a map? just money thrown
away. Tobo, you and Ida take Arabella between
you that she mayn't be lost in the crowd. Emma,
give one hand to ma and one to me."

"And you mind your pocket-book, Sylvester," said
Mrs. Paragreen — "are you sure you have got it?"

"All safe, my dear," replied Mr. Paragreen, tapping
one of the numerous pockets by which his coat was
honey-combed. Crossing over, they made for the
Succursale, through the wide open portals of which,
however, they could not perceive any of that dense
crowd they had anticipated. Mr. Paragreen was
most agreeably surprised at not being asked for
money at the door, and with great gusto returned to
his purse the six francs he had had all ready in his
hand, observing, as he did so — "In justice to our

French neighbours, we must allow that almost everything can be seen in Paris gratis."

The Succursale was by no means remarkable for the grandeur of its architecture, nor for the richness or rarity of the articles exhibited. The building consisted of a narrow long room, supported by wooden pillars, and terminating in a raised circular-shaped platform. Four rows of stalls, the size of Punch's show, containing china, glass, toys, cutlery, ormoulu jewelry, straw-work, haberdashery, &c., extended from one end of the space to the other, forming three alleys or lanes, where visitors could perambulate at their leisure. The roof being of glass, there was plenty of light.

Though the Paragreens' expectations were not highly raised, having been forewarned by Alderman Joliffe that the Paris Exhibition was nothing wonderful, still the reality fell very short of even what they had imagined. Tobo asked, quite surlily, what the devil the French could mean by enticing people to come to such a penny peep-show of a place? Why, the Crystal Palace would hold no end of such trumpery holes one on the top of the other; and Mrs. Paragreen declared it was only what *she* had expected from the very beginning. Mr. Paragreen, who was in one of his patronizing moods, contended that they were too difficult to please — it was small, certainly, but uncommonly well arranged. "We must recollect we are in France and not in England, my dears. I said to Joliffe, when we were speaking on this very subject — My dear sir, says I, they do what they can, you know, and their efforts ought rather to be encouraged than otherwise. It is not fair to exact from an infant learning to walk, what you have a right to expect from a vigorous adult. Now industry, manufactures, and all that in France are still in the cradle. As to me, I confess this modesty, this want of all attempt at rivalling us, pleases me much. Now what fault can you find with this Rotunda, or such straw work as this?" — (putting up his eye-glass, and stooping to examine a roll of ornamental straw.) "It is not to be despised, I assure you. Bong, très bong," added Mr. Paragreen to the owner of the stall. "Ha! a buffet! I see," continued he of Eden Villa, in the tone of a man recognising an old friend; "excellent! the wants of visitors most properly attended to. Would you like a bun, Emma, and you, Bella, what do you say? will you have a glass of wine or some lemonade, Dora?"

Thus discoursing, observing, and eating buns, they continued their tour of inspection; Mr. Paragreen pertinaciously finding something at every step to admire, or approve of; asking the price of this and that, and, as was his duty as a practical man, noting down the answer in his memorandum-book, but never buying a pennyworth in spite of the repeated and rather pressing invitations he received to do so. Mr. Paragreen liked the locality, and felt quite at home in it.

Their number, their round hats, the free and easy manner with which they wandered about, surveying everything as if they had bought and paid for it, something eccentric in their gait, gestures, and garments, made the Paragreens the centre of attraction to the few scores of loungers present, but chiefly to the holders of stalls, who were more amused than flattered by the unusual minute examination bestowed on their wares. By the time the Macedonian phalanx were off on their third journey, round the Succursale, a species of acquaintanceship, by dint of gazing at each other, had sprung up between the family and the Exhibitors in general; and, in especial, with a young, fat, jolly-looking fellow, who never failed to salute their advent in front of his stand by deferential bows and smiles.

Mrs. Paragreen rather suspected he was making fun of them — but Mr. Paragreen pooh-poohed the notion — observing that the French were such sociable odd beings, that they must needs converse by nods and smiles as well as with their tongues. To this particular jovial friend of his, Mr. Paragreen applied, whenever he had any doubts to solve, or complaints to make, always meeting from the Frenchman an obliging explanation, or a still more obliging sympathy. Mr. Paragreen learned, for instance, through this channel of information, that the "Machinerie," as he designated the Machinery Department, was in a Galerie au bord de l'Eau "là bas dans cette direction," and that the English goods, which were nowhere to be seen, had been placed, by the jealousy of the French Commission, in a "bâtiment où n'allait personne." Such unfair treatment had drawn forth a burst of indignation from the questioner, softened down, however, by the reflection, that it was the best acknowledgment, after all, of England's suporiority. Having also searched, without success, for the Crown Jewels, which they all knew were in the Rotunda, and for which six pair of eyes had been, for the last half hour, peeping into every hole and corner, Mr. Paragreen once more accosted his kind informant with "Les Diamangs du Couronne, s'il vous plait?"

"Ah! les Diamans de la Couronne?" with a sad shake of the head from the jolly fellow, "pas encore arrivés des Tuileries — no komme from Tuileries."

"Commong from Tuileries?" asked Mr. Paragreen.

"Tous les soirs — hall evening, the Diamans portés aux Tuileries — Diamans very costive, quinze millions — l'Empereur put dem sous clef." Here the rogue drew a key from his pocket, and turned it in an imaginary lock.

"How mean and stingy!" cried Mrs. Paragreen, catching the Frenchman's meaning, and quite angry.

"Well I must own it is shabby," pronounced Mr.

Paragreen gravely; he pondered a moment, then laying his stumpy forefinger on the fat man's arm, slowly articulated, "Pas bong, monseer, miserabel, Anglais plus generousse." So saying, he turned and walked away, just in time not to see the jolly traitor roaring with laughter till the tears rolled down his face.

"Galerie Bour de Loue, s'il vous plait?" asked Mr. Paragreen, as he emerged from the Succursale of a passer-by. "Galerie quoi?" asked the person so addressed. "Galerie de Machineries, s'il vous plait?"

"Tout droit, au fond de l'Avenue, vous la voyez d'ici," said the man, his gesture more explanatory to the Paragreens than his words.

Our sight-seers had not gone fifty steps in the direction pointed out, before they lighted upon a set of masons, lying on the ground in front of a half-finished house, a good number of whom were eating slices of melon. Mr. Paragreen came to one of his sudden halts, and holding out his hand, as if taking aim at the prostrate figures, he remarked with great feeling, — "Is it not sad to think that so large a proportion, I might with truth say the immense majority, of the French nation, understanding by that the artisans and mechanics, are forced to live on pumpkin? I had heard so, but I own that till this instant, when I see the fact with my own eyes, I always thought it a traveller's story. Now this is one of the advantages of visiting foreign countries. Travelling, Tobo, my dear boy, I speak more to you than the girls, because you are more likely to move about than they are — travelling, I repeat, is a sort of — practical — what shall I call it? — a sort of practical — not theory, you know — in short, a most instructive thing. Remark how thin these poor men are," continued Mr. Paragreen, taking as cool a survey of the working people as if they had been their own stones and bricks; "I have not the least doubt the difference of food has much to do with the greater muscular development, and higher spirit of our own countrymen, — for I believe no one has ever denied that one Englishman is worth four Frenchmen, — a superiority which ought not to make us proud, but thankful to that Providence which grants abundance to our land, and ordained us to be the first nation in the world."

"Suppose we wish them joy of their pumpkin, and go on," exclaimed Mrs. Paragreen. "I don't know where your eyes are, but I can see that these people are looking at us in a very improper manner."

"Fancy, all fancy, Dora, I can't believe anything of the kind," replied Mr. Paragreen.

However, it was no fancy of dear Dora's, but very sober reality. The melon-eaters did not at all relish the close scrutiny of which they were the objects; and their grins and grimaces, significant of impatience, caused Mr. Paragreen to follow his wife's lead, though he persisted in murmuring, "Poor things, they mean no harm, I daresay, but we won't disturb their humble meal."

When the Paragreens at length reached the Annexe, a new surprise awaited them, in the turnstile impeding their farther progress; and Mr. Paragreen was further greatly taken aback and displeased by a demand for six francs, as the price of admission for himself and his party. He paid, however, without making any objection, as he perceived that every person going in laid down a franc.

"Now this is just such a piece of inconsistency

as only Frenchmen are capable of;" quoth the disturbed little man, — "they give you free access to the principal Exhibition, and then make you pay for the secondary thing." This was not the only incongruity which Mr. Paragreen was yet to lay at the door of the French nation on that day; for he no sooner caught sight of the distant spot indicating the termination of the Gallery — such a perspective line as brought at once a conviction of its extraordinary length, and of the enormous amount and variety of machinery it must contain — than he broke forth on the same theme, and descanted with warmth on the ridiculous disproportion between the main building and this its mere accessory. Did the French want to make believe, forsooth, that they were so in advance of all the rest of the world in machinery and engineering, that they required for that single department ten times the room that had been allotted for manufactures and commerce?

By degrees the little gentleman's heat cooled as he observed that a very ample space was conceded for the display of the machinery of his country; and he said he was free to confess that this looked like fair play. It is not our intention to enter into any particulars as to what most attracted the attention of our family, or called forth their admiration. We shall only note that they stood a long time before every sewing machine, and repeatedly partook of the hot coffee and chocolate out of the same urns — according to the label on them — from which the Emperor and his royal guests had deigned to have cups filled, and had praised as excellent. They paid great attention also to the carriage department; Mr. Paragreen very busy comparing notes of those which had the prices marked with those that had not; and to arrive at the knowledge of the cost of these last, bustling away to the different bureaux, a worry and a trouble to every one he fell in with. The very largest engines became also objects of his inquisitiveness; he must be made to understand all their drift and power, and the expense of them.

So gratified were the family by their inspection, that it was only a fresh outcry for buns from Emma and Arabella, which made the seniors wonder what o'clock it could be, and caused Mr. Paragreen to pull out his watch. "Bless my heart! we must make haste or we shall be too late for the table d'hôte; it's five o'clock, by all that's good!" So away they hurried by the first door they met, and reached their Hotel, without deviating from the right road, in high spirits, and in capital cue for their dinner.

CHAPTER IV.

Hero-Worship.

THE Company staying at the hotel were already assembled, and busily at work in the dining-room, into which our Peckham couple and their offspring were ushered; not the common one, as the waiter informed them, but the "reserved dining-room."

A little awed by the silence pervading this apartment, in strong contrast to the hilarious sounds issuing from one opposite, and which, from the inscription of "Salle à manger" over its door, was probably the unreserved or plebeian eating-room; the new-comers seated themselves, on the chairs destined for them, at the lower end of the table, — a trying performance at any time, whatever the assurance of the actors, but especially so when, as in the present case, it takes place under the combined fire of twenty pairs of eyes. Mr. Paragreen tried to cloak his embarrassment by observing to Mrs. Paragreen, in a half-whisper, that "it was really a very pretty room," — a remark that brought upon him all the eyes again, and a frown of great severity from the lady on his left.

Though quite at a loss to account for the general animosity displayed towards him and his, Mr. Paragreen made up his mind to leave the mystery unsolved, and to eat his dinner, — a good example closely followed by his wife and children. Scarcely two minutes had passed in this agreeable occupation, when, as if by magic, all the tongues were unloosed, the present clatter being as unaccountable to Mr. Paragreen as the stillness that had preceded it. Little by little, as happens at table-d'hôtes, the ice once broken, conversation spread and became general, — that is, every one talked, the Upper Endians among themselves, and the Lower Endians among themselves. They were all English, at least all spoke English; and the prevailing topic was naturally the Paris Exhibition.

Mr. Paragreen watched his opportunity, and, during a moment's lull, audibly observed, that, "though prepared for a disappointment by a friend of his, Mr. Joliffe of Hackney, — he meant Alderman Joliffe, a cousin of his wife, — well, — though prepared for many wants, and for much meagerness, still he must say, with regret say, that things were worse than he believed possible. Compare the London and Paris Exhibition! why, where could any one find a point of comparison?"

This opinion received the assent of all present, and conquered for the speaker the goodwill of his hearers, who, to say the least, had not shewn any prepossession in Mr. Paragreen's favour at first sight.

"So small," continued Mr. Paragreen, emboldened by success.

"Such a trumpery concern altogether," chimed in Mrs. Paragreen.

"Trumpery concern, madam!" repeated a gentleman in a white cravat and gold spectacles, sitting exactly opposite the lady; "do you know, madam, that the space covered by your trumpery concern amounts to 140,000 square metres, — just 45,000 square metres, metres, madam, more than our London Exhibition, — and that the number of Exhibitors in this trumpery concern is not less than

25,000, seven thousand more than there were in England?"

"I should never have thought it possible," answered Mr. Paragreen overwhelmed, and rather crestfallen, "even taking in that monstrous machine gallery, so ridiculously out of all proportion with the main building."

"I beg your pardon," said the gifted individual in spectacles, who knew all areas, all dates, all numbers, and the length, depth, and width of all things, "the Annexe, which you call the Machine Gallery, measures *pre*-cisely —"

A scream from Mrs. Paragreen cut short the speaker's calculations, and made every one start and look at that lady. "It's frogs, Mr. Paragreen! — frogs!" said Mrs. Dora, jumping up horrified at the dish presented to her, and so jogging the waiter's arm, that he landed some of the obnoxious viands on the table-cloth. This asseveration excited a great consternation, particularly among the fair sex, and elicited some cries of "Abominable!" from the uglier gender. The waiter swore by all the gods that the dish was innocent of the charge, and consisted of a fricassée of pigeons, (which, by the bye, Mr. Paragreen translated into sacrificed pigeons,) and to prove his assertion, the offended attendant carried the dish for inspection to a dark-visaged, dark-mustachioed gentleman, occupying the post of honour — that is, the head of the table — who, after a glance said, "De fait, it is pigeon, any one can see," — a sentence received with a hum that expressed satisfaction and gratitude towards the utterer.

"Well, sir, I was about to give you," said the gold-spectacled dealer in facts, beginning where he had left off, as soon as quiet was restored, "I was about to give you a figure, an authentic figure—"

"I can't say anything about figures, sir," interrupted Mr. Paragreen, "but one thing I do know, and stick to — that is, that the Paris Exhibition is an inferior business, and precious ill regulated — upon that point I hope you don't mean to contradict me, sir. Allow me one moment — what can you say in defence of the charge of a franc a-head for admission into the Annex, as you call it, while the entrance to the main building is gratis? I say it is just like the French — no heads for business—"

"Who told you such nonsense?" asked a dashing young man, a London chemist's assistant, whose well-curled hair and whiskers retained a strong odour of the hairdresser's irons.

"Sir," said Mr. Paragreen with some dignity, "I am indebted to nobody for my information, I made the discovery myself."

"Then you haven't been to the right place," remarked the druggist, "there is but one building and one fee, my good sir."

Mr. Paragreen, who began to have some misgivings of his own, was willing to let the subject drop, but his ill-inspired better half had a weight on her mind, which unburden she must.

"They are a shabby set from beginning to end, that I always thought," began Mrs. Paragreen sententiously, "but they are meaner than I gave them credit for."

This sentiment was received with universal stares.

"Don't you call it meanness, sir," continued the lady, nothing daunted, and turning her eyes full on gold-spectacles, "for the head of the country to be having his diamonds carried back and forwards to the Tuileries, and locking them up himself every day? that's what I call down-right shabby."

Oh ohs, and half suppressed laughter sounded on all sides, subsiding, however, into silence, on the gentleman at the top of the table inquiring what was the matter. On being told, this good-looking individual laughed long and loudly, the signal for laughs from every one present except Mr. and Mrs. Paragreen, who, by dint of striving to prove their case, of cross-questioning, and being cross-questioned, stood convicted at last of having mistaken a bazaar for the Palais de l'Industrie.

The next subject of discussion was Ristori. Have you seen Ristori? Yes — no — a man or woman? — is she French? No — a great actress — an Italian. Oh!! This last oh! from Mr. Paragreen, seemed to imply that it would have been better for her if she had been a Frenchwoman.

"We must go and see this Ristoar," observed he, Mæcenas-like, over Emma's head to his wife.

"Of course," said the lady, fully concurring in such a necessity.

"Go and see her in Mirra, Sir." "By all means

see her in Mary Stuart, Madam — beats Rachel all to nothing in that part." This last was the judgment delivered by the young chemist. A fat, vapid blonde — a literary character seated by his side — simpered forth, "Oh! Rachel!" but was overcrowed by Mrs. Paragreen saying in her loud way, "We saw *her* in London: — my cousin took a box — nothing so wonderful about her that I could find out."

"Rachel," pursued the fat blonde, pursing up her mouth, and with a slight bend towards Mrs. Paragreen, "is only fitted for a French audience; — to me there is something so unchristian-like about her acting, it was really painful to see her in Phædre — her love is the love of a pagan."

"Pardon me, Madam," said a gentleman who up to this time had not opened his lips, "but surely it would be much out of character, if, in representing a pagan heroine, Rachel gave her the attributes of a Christian."

This remark was offered in that hesitating tone which characterizes shy people, and therefore passed quite unheeded. The world belongs to those who take it, my dear friends, says an old Italian proverb, and the proverb is right.

"Give me Jenny Lind," went on the vapid lady, as if no one had spoken. ("Ah! Jenny Lind!!" parenthesized a bald round-headed gentleman from the other end of the table, nodding enthusiastically at the speaker.) "Give me Jenny Lind," and the fair speaker threw her eyes up as if asking the ceiling for the boon. "Is there such another in the world? — the perfection of art and nature — nature and art so cunningly blended in her that you have actress — singer — passionate woman — gentlewoman — Christian woman — the Beautiful, therefore the True — in short, the —" here the speaker's feelings spoiled her climax.

A salvo of syncopated ahs! ehs! ihs! ohs! broke forth from all the ladies; all the gentlemen striking an emphatic chord of "charming!" all except the shy one, who gave a discordant bass note that sounded strangely like "humbug." The dark gentleman at the top of the table bowed to the fair oratress.

"Rachel and Ristori," said he slowly, in a sort of

general address, (all tongues were hushed, all clatter of forks and knives ceased, all heads turned towards the speaker,) Rachel and Ristori, it cannot be denied, have each uncommon powers — one has this, the other that quality — but, as the lady just now so feelingly and clearly expressed it, they both want *that* which makes the great charm of Jenny Lind— a soul — a Christian soul."

Pitt or Fox, in their palmiest days, never had such an oratorical triumph; the ladies clasped their hands; many eyes were moist, and handkerchiefs appeared; the male portion drummed on the table, making every glass tinkle for joy. The shy dissentient alone drew in his breath with a hissing sound.

"Who is the gentleman that spoke last?" asked Mr. Paragreen of his neighbour, the lady with the severe frown.

"His Highness the Prince of ——. What is he Prince of, my dear?" whispered she to her husband, who was on her other flank.

"Hush!" whispered back the husband, "the Prince is looking this way, he will hear you."

"Prince of Something, Somewhere — a victim — Russia," murmured the lady in Mr. Paragreen's ear.

"Bless my heart!" exclaimed our hero, his face reddening — "how awkward not to know these things in time!" — and he began tucking away the ends of his black cravat, — "I would have put on a white neckcloth, at least."

"Oh!" continued his informant, "the Prince is very affable, and not at all ceremonious."

The tremendous intelligence was forthwith telegraphed to Mrs. Paragreen, who was so stunned that she felt an all-overness and very hot in the back, as if she were going to faint — at least so she afterwards declared — but could, nevertheless, summon presence of mind enough to impart the news, in an awe-struck whisper, to the rest of the family. So they had been seated for an' hour at the same table with a Prince, a real live Prince, and knew nothing about it — and been shown up too in such a ridiculous light. Imagine yourself in the place of our friends, dear reader, and then you may judge of the contention of feelings racking Mr. and Mrs. Paragreen's breasts. Had it been only the Prince of Wales, or the Prince of Prussia, or the Prince of Sweden, or the Prince of anything you can put a name to, or append a figure denoting so many thousand square miles, and so many millions of inhabitants, the shock would have been less. But Prince of Something! Somewhere! the Unknown, the Indefinite, the Illimitable, the Unfathomable — only think!!

The senior Paragreens, from this moment, tried hard to atone for their past irreverence towards the august presence, by those manifold silent tokens of obsequiousness with which well-bred independent people strive to propitiate a superior — and never did sunflowers turn more constantly and amorously to the great Luminary of Day, than the owners of Eden Villa to that sun which gilded and hallowed the reserved dining-room of the Unicorn Hotel.

"It is not etiquette, I suppose, to leave before His Highness?" inquired Mr. Paragreen softly, of his lady neighbour.

"Oh! dear, *no.*" The emphasis placed on these two words seemed to intimate, that if one of the party had suddenly died of apoplexy, the corpse

could not have been removed, unless the Prince had
left the table. Mr. Paragreen's query had been
suggested by the circumstance of the shy gentleman
making an attempt to escape at the end of dinner,
and being caught, and held by the skirts of the coat,
by the persons on each side of him, and warmly re-
monstrated with.

In the meantime, the Prince was grinning sweetly
to this lady, and then to that, — another biscuit? —
another glass of wine? — not another biscuit? — no
more wine? — Well — then His Highness may get
up, and move to the mantelpiece, against which he
leans in a classical attitude, one hand shoved daintily
within his waistcoat, his right leg picturesquely
crossed over the left. His Highness's personal appearance is certainly most prepossessing, — no wonder the
ladies dote on him. He is young, tall, and well
made, — his manners are easy and condescending
without affectation, — his smile patronizing, yet not
haughty, — his toilette irreproachable, and quite free
from finery; a brown dress-coat with velvet collar,
the sleeves so wide as to give a peep of the finest
and whitest of linen; light fancy trousers; open-

worked black silk stockings, and patent-leather pumps; — in short, as trim, tidy, and tasty, as if he were just about to appear on the stage, in the character of a man of fashion. Now seen between his rich black satin tie, and the velvet collar of his coat, now lost under a white waistcoat of a simple military cut, meander two broad blue ribbons, at the lower junction of which you can discover, when the wearer leans forward, something glittering, — the insignia of one favourite order, among innumerable others His Highness has a right to wear.

It is in the attitude just designated as classical, that His Highness usually holds his little levee, and receives little homages, while coffee is being served. The privileged mortals who have the honour of a seat at the upper section of the table, near His Highness, — an honour only conferred by seniority, except in the case of the Honourable Ananias Smallwhey and his three charming daughters, who have made the acquaintance of His Highness in London, — these privileged mortals, we say, group themselves to the right and left of the Prince, just as we see, at the opera, the grandees and high dignitaries group themselves round Mario or Lablache, with this only difference, that the present grandees do not sing. While this is going on, the less fortunate occupants of the lower section, drawn up in a row on the opposite sides of the table, move slowly towards the chimney, make their bows or courtesies, and then retire to the rear of the privileged body-guard. This is the usual moment for the presentation of new-comers.

The Paragreens looked most perplexed, but help was at hand in the shape of the bald round-headed Jenny Lindite. "Wish to be introduced, eh? Very well, — what name? Paragreen. Good, — make three bows, and don't speak first. Where is the other gentleman?" The other gentleman, the shy one, was nowhere to be found, and was given up. Great is the flutter of heart of our worthy Paragreen, as, preceded by the self-elected Master of Ceremonies, and followed by his palpitating family, he moves, and they move, towards the august presence, — the centre of attraction to all eyes.

His Highness returns bow for bow to Mr. Paragreen, — waves off all apologetic explanation, — advances with regal grace towards Mrs. Paragreen, — compliments Papa and Mamma on their "beautiful" family, (with a condescending stare at pretty Ida, who blushes portentously.) "Such a charming addition to our small social circle," says His Highness.

"You belong to a country, Sir," turning full on little Paragreen, on whom he looks down from his six feet superiority, — "you belong to a country, Madam, (all ears are on the alert, all necks on the stretch), which, allow me to say, is entitled to my best wishes. It is on England, Sir, on England *alone*, that I rely for the vindication of my rights, trampled upon by wanton tyranny — and that wanton tyranny, Sir, a cousin; Sir, a cousin, (profound sensation.) But let us turn to a more agreeable theme. I shall never forget the words which dropped from Royal lips at Windsor — was it at Windsor or at Osborne? — Prince — these were the words — you may depend on England, and on England's Queen," (renewed syncopation of ihs! ohs! uhs!) "Did I say 'Queen?' I regret having, in the warmth of my feelings, named a name which I ought reverently to have withheld — I mean by this, Sir and Madam, that you are welcome, very welcome. I like and respect English people. I have many friends among your countrymen. And when, on my first coming to Paris, another august person — you will pardon my not being more explicit — offered me rooms in the Tuil——, no matter where, why did I respectfully decline this honour? Because I feel nowhere so at home, as I do among the English." (Murmurs of applause.) "I hope I shall have the pleasure of seeing more of you." And, with a slight bow, His Highness returns to the mantelpiece, and gracefully sips the remains of his cup of Mocha.

Now follows a dissection of the Court Circular of the day. Her Majesty going to Versailles during the week, a grand fête there — the King of Piedmont cannot come to Paris, and why not — the Grand Duchess has had a headache. His Highness raises his eyebrows and shakes his head with sadness; but, at this point of interest, the company is interrupted by the appearance of a long-bearded servant, gorgeously dressed in a half Eastern garb, bearing a salver, with a huge despatch on it. A gentleman in black lifts it off the salver, and hands it to His Highness, who begs pardon with a sweeping bow, breaks the seal, and reads: —

"Ladies and Gentlemen, I must now leave you. Though dethroned, I have still some state affairs" (with a smile) "which call for my attention — so, ladies and gentlemen, adieu!" And followed by the richly-draped attendant, and the gentleman in black, amid bows, courtesies, and smiles, exit our illustrious Highness — shaking his sides with laughter, perhaps? — Not at all; — erect, composed, majestic, leaving behind him, as it were, a track of glory. So the curtain drops.

Ladies and gentlemen, we say in our turn, do not denounce the picture as overdrawn. Such farces are performed any day of this enlightened nineteenth century in Paris, in London, at Vienna, no matter where the stage, amid the applause of crowded audiences, and to the final discomfiture of credulous innkeepers, purveyors, tradesmen, and such small fry. Yes, such baits are offered, and eagerly swallowed; and will be offered and swallowed to the end of time, till —— the bells of our fool's cap give warning that this is neither the hour nor the place for moralizing.

CHAPTER V.

Short but Instructive.

"WELL, Mr. Paragreen, I hope you are satisfied, — thanks to your famous bump of locality, a fine début you have made us make before His Royal Highness! It's a miracle that, with such a grand protuberance, you can keep a hat on your head, — I wonder at it, — I do indeed." (Mr. Paragreen drooped his offending head.) "His Highness must set us down for a parcel of thorough blockheads. You are enough to vex a saint, that you are!"

With running this tilt at her husband, Mrs. Paragreen varied the monotony of their ascent to their garrets.

"The Prince is too much of a man of the world, too sensible, my dear," said Mr. Paragreen, in a conciliatory voice, "not to make every allowance for strangers. I plead guilty to having blundered, but grant me the benefit of extenuating circumstances.

I defy any one not to have been deceived by such an unaccountable concatenation of ——."

"No — no one but a self-conceited, obstinate booby like you would ever have been so taken in. If it hadn't been for your maudlin nonsense about France and Frenchmen, and your genius for being made a fool of by the first jackanapes you come across, Tobo and I would have found out fast enough that we were wrong. I suspected it all along. But you must always have your own way, — you always know best, you know, — you can't be mistaken in people."

The allusion to his friend in the Succursale seemed to offer to the strategic little man a favourable opportunity for a diversion, at which he eagerly caught.

"As for that good-for-nothing puppy, who made game of us," he said, blustering, "he had better keep out of my way; for, by jingo, if ever I catch him, I'll squeeze his love for bamboozling the English out of his body, — that he may depend upon, as sure as my name is ——."

"For goodness' sake, Mr. Paragreen, let's have no more of your tomfooleries — buy a map of Paris, and let us find our way by it, that's the best thing you can do. All we must hope is, that our ridiculous mistakes won't reach Peckham. I have no wish to be a laughing-stock at home as well as abroad;" and so saying, the lady went into an inner room, banging the door after her.

"Your mother may say what she likes," remarked Mr. Paragreen, left alone with his children, "but as for me, I really don't regret the time we spent in the Succursale. Besides the advantage of our now having a point of comparison to go by, I declare on my honour, that I learned more of French character and manners in those two hours, than from all the travels I ever read, put together. You see, Tobo, my boy, a practical man is like — what shall I say? — like a bee, a busy bee, drawing honey from every flower; he turns to account even disappointments, looking on them as warnings, that the greatest prudence and foresight do not exempt him from the common lot of humanity."

"May I ask if we are going to stay in this stifling place the whole evening?" asked Mrs. Paragreen, sulkily, as she emerged from the recesses of the inner room.

Mr. Paragreen cheerfully proposed a walk to the Champs Elysées, as the best place to get a breath of fresh air. Mrs. Paragreen feared that it might be too fatiguing for Emma and Arabella, who declared they could walk any distance.

"We shall find plenty of seats there, my dear," observed Mr. Paragreen; "and if the girls are tired, we can take a coach home — there's no lack of carriages in Paris, whatever else is wanting."

With this understanding off they set, three abreast, as usual, to the Champs Elysées, to enjoy the cool of the evening, as the phrase goes, but in reality to be choked by the dust, and jostled and hustled by a motley crowd.

The fine proportions and tasteful decorations of the Place de la Concorde, did not produce much effect on our sight-seers; the youthful part of whom, however, were surprised into uttering little cries of delight, by the beautiful chestnut trees of the Terrace of the Tuileries, and by the fountains playing on each side of the obelisk. At sight of this, Mr. Paragreen brought up all sail, standing to calculate how many inches higher or lower than the monument of London it might be; scrutinizing the characters and figures inscribed on the granite with so knowing an air, that the still sulky Mrs. Paragreen asked him whether he wished to make the passers-by believe that he understood "herryglyphs." "Heroglyphs," corrected Mr. Paragreen sedately. "Herry, or hero doesn't much signify," retorted Mrs. Paragreen tartly, "it ends in *iph*, I know."

The amateurs of the fresh evening air were so numerous, and the space allotted to pedestrians so much encroached upon by the occupants of chairs, that Mr. Paragreen saw the necessity of modifying the order of march of the little phalanx, and gave the order to move in twos; Ida and Tobo in the first rank, Emma and Arabella supporting them, while he and Mrs. Paragreen, in the rear, represented the heavy artillery. This division of forces gave rise to three separate dialogues, some scraps of which we caught, and wrote down.

Mr. Paragreen. — "Very pleasant indeed! a little over-crowded, though — no low company — one might really fancy one's-self in a drawing-room; all people of a certain rank, I take it."

Mrs. Paragreen. — "As far as dress is concerned, it is very well — but I am sure I can't see any of the French grace everybody talks of, nor a pretty face either. There are lots of carriages, but the half of them are hackney-coaches — it spoils the *coupe d'œil*, don't it? — they ought not to be allowed. These sort of things are much better managed in England."

Mr. Paragreen thinks they are. "The French have no aristocracy, you know; no real aristocracy," (with a sad shake of the head.)

Mrs. Paragreen. — "So much the worse for them, so much the worse for them. I wouldn't give a pin for a country without an aristocracy. I wonder whether the Prince is here. Is that him in the carriage and four, with an outrider?"

Mr. Paragreen. — "No, don't you see there's only a lady in it? Somebody belonging to the Imperial Court, I suppose."

Mrs. Paragreen. — "Perhaps that Princess — what's her name? — His Highness was talking of — Ho! the Grand Duchess of Bagdad."

Mr. Paragreen. — "Baden, Baden, my dear."

Mrs. Paragreen. — "Lor, Mr. Paragreen, how you do worry about trifles, Baden or Bagdad is much the same — you know who I mean, very well. After all, it was a piece of luck our not getting in at that Seegong. We might never have known His Highness but for that; so I don't mind a bit now having had to sleep in the streets, in them what d'ye call 'ems — so handsome, so accomplished."

Mr. Paragreen. — "Bears the stamp of royal birth on his countenance, and in his manners."

Mrs. Paragreen. — "And so affable too! — What a monkey-looking little monster!"

Mr. Paragreen. — "Who? the Prince?"

Mrs. Paragreen. — "Good gracious, no — there, that man on the grey horse, who looks so mightily pleased to see us. I daresay he could present us at the Court here."

Mr. Paragreen. — "Who, my dear? — oh! the Prince, I have no doubt he could."

Mrs. Paragreen. — "You had better call and leave a card on him. I should so enjoy getting to Court; it would be as good as poison to Mrs. Jones.

Do you see that black and yellow livery? — very bad taste."

Mr. Paragreen. — "No accounting you know, Dora my dear, for tastes — eh! when you swore for better for worse — eh?" (Silence.) "I trust and hope, and almost expect, that we shall receive an invitation to the Embassy. I think it is our due. Ha! Exposition des Fleurs — a flower show: we must go there of course by daylight. Bless my heart! what a crowd! I am half stifled. What's that building over the way there, I wonder, with so many flags!"

Mrs. Paragreen. — "Can't you see? — Palace of Industry. I am sure its name and itself are big enough. There's the British flag — it makes me feel all I don't know how, to look at it hanging there so far from home."

Mr. Paragreen. — (hugging his wife's arm.) — "It does, it does, my dear. You are right, that's the real Exhibition — not so grand after all, but rather neat."

Mrs. Paragreen. — (with a good-natured smile.) — "We shan't lose our way to the Exhibition again, now we have the British lion for a guide."

Mr. Paragreen. — (keeping the plump arm tightly within his own.) — "I hope not. You are rather hasty, my dear little woman, but your heart is a treasure, it is."

Mrs. Paragreen. — "Gracious me! I am in a perfect state of perspiration."

Emma. — "What a number of booths! it's like a fair! Oh! there's Punch, I declare."

Arabella. — "Look at those roundabouts — how nice! The boys have horses to ride, and the girls go in boats. I would rather ride, wouldn't you?"

Emma. — "Oh, Bella, just see what a lovely little carriage drawn by goats! I wish mamma would give us a drive in it."

Arabella. — "Don't ask. It cost so much to bring us all here, papa said. I wonder what that man is selling: he has got a string of glasses round his neck, and something like an organ covered with red velvet on his back. Oh! I see what it is now, it's a pump full of lemonade."

Emma. — "How curious to hear every one talking

French! — children less than me — it seems impossible they can understand it."

Arabella. — "Look at that lady in white before us. She sticks out more than Ma or Da, doesn't she?"

Emma. — "Yes. When we are grown up we may wear as much bustle as we choose."

Ida. — "How gay and pleasant! isn't it, Tobo?"

Tobo. — "And so horribly hot and dusty too! I hope you don't mean to say you think it equal to Hyde Park and the Serpentine. There isn't a carriage here to compare to any of the grand London ones."

Ida. — "Now look at that one passing, and that other with the big grey horses. I am sure they are quite perfect."

Tobo. — "Perfect, indeed! — poor little Da! she does not know much about horse-flesh — how should she? I'll tell you what I *do* like though, Da — it's the Café Chantangs — there — don't the girls look like a nosegay of roses? It would be much pleasanter to sit and hear them sing, and have some beer, than all this pushing and squeezing."

Ida. — "Oh, Tobo!"

Tobo. — "Well, what's there vulgar in beer? How short and ugly all these Frenchmen are! What does that nasty little puppy mean, I say?" (looking defiant.)

Ida. — "Don't, Tobo, don't stare so at people, you always do."

Tobo. — "I won't be bullied by any one, least of all by a French frog. What the deuce make them wear a tuft of hair on their chins like a goat's beard? I hate it, don't you, Da?"

Ida. — "I don't think it is ugly when it is soft and silky, and not too big."

Tobo. — "Like that fellow's, I suppose, who is staring his eyes out at you, eh, Ida?"

Ida — (blushing scarlet.) — "Oh, Tobo! what nonsense!"

Tobo's remark applied to a smart little individual, whose light whiskers and tuft on the chin, expressive glances and sweet voice, had for some time captivated pretty Miss Ida's attention. But how could she know anything about his voice if he were alone, as was the case? exclaims some hypercritical reader. Ah, simple reader! for simple you must be not to know all the resources a throng like this can furnish to a love-smitten swain. The honest truth then is, that the shepherd in question, not contented with pressing his hands together as if squeezing an imaginary lemon, or with sucking the gilt knob of his cane in the most sentimental way at Miss Paragreen, had made a pretence of being drifted by the swelling tide of walkers close to the young lady, and once there had sighed in her ear a "Bi-yu-ti-ful!" so sweet, that the most mellifluous of flutes could never have come up to it. Now, when a damsel of twenty, whose heart has not yet spoken, hears herself pronounced "Biyutiful" in this mysterious way by a trim, good-looking, well-fed, well-clad gentleman of eight-and-twenty or so, it naturally throws her into a flutter of spirits. And if the admirer's manner borders on the theatrical — if the bows of his narrow neck-tie project so far right and left as to suggest the image of a walking T— what does it matter? Is it perchance the most unaffected and truest actors on the stage of love who are the most successful, we should like to know?

Meanwhile our family had reached the Rond Point to have a view of the Arc de l'Etoile, which they had entirely overlooked during the morning's hot chase after the Exhibition. In this they were foiled, however, for it was already dark. Emma and Arabella whispered that they were tired.

"We'll get chairs, then," said Mr. Paragreen; "upon my word, I shall not be sorry to sit down myself, I am so hot. How do you feel, Dora?"

Mrs. Paragreen agreed that she should also like a rest. They therefore retraced their steps in search of chairs — namely, of six unoccupied chairs. Now they could almost as easily have found six vacant thrones: one of the peculiar charms of Paris during the Exhibition being, that whenever you particularly wanted a chair, a coach, or a seat in a Café, Restaurant, or Theatre, no matter which, or where, or what, you were sure not to find it.

"Very odd, though," exclaimed Mr. Paragreen.

"Not odd at all," replied Dora peevishly; "from the moment you said there would be plenty of seats

I ought to have known that the case was hopeless."

"But, Dora, dear —"

"Don't dear me, pray, but beckon to a coach, and let us get home as fast as we can; there's plenty of *them*, luckily."

Mr. Paragreen bellowed "cochère," at the innumerable vehicles passing, without making any distinction — it was too dark indeed to see which were public and which were private — but to no purpose; everything on wheels was either full, or unattainable. Most of the coachmen went on their way without appearing to notice the Englishman's urgent call, a few more civil telegraphed a negative. Poor Mr. Paragreen, the most disconcerted of men, turned toward his wife, who sympathizingly, and not at all sarcastically, remarked, "No want of coaches in Paris, whatever else is wanting, eh?"

"But, my dear Dora, is it my fault if they are engaged?"

At this crisis, little Emma dropped on the pavement crying, and Arabella followed her example — the children could not, and would not keep on their feet any longer. Extreme evils call for extreme remedies. Mr. Paragreen took up Arabella in his arms, ordered Tobo in a tone that admitted of no reply, to carry Emma, and thus they trudged back, Æneas-like, to the Hotel — Tobo grumbling and stumbling; Mr. Paragreen panting like a high-pressure engine; Mrs. Paragreen inveighing against her husband, against the good-for-nothing little hussies, against the Exhibition, and against Paris, while poor Ida limped by her side, crying like a child.

CHAPTER VI.

The Exhibition.

We are happy to begin the present chapter with a more agreeable sketch from nature than that with which it was our painful duty to close the last. On the sofa, in the soi-disant salon, the largest of the three small rooms allotted to our family, sits Mr. Paragreen. Ida, with one of her hands in his, is on one side of him, and Tobo on the other; Emma kneels on the parental lap, wiping away with her own little pocket-handkerchief, the effects of bodily exertion on a close August morning from the good man's brow; and Arabella, who has squeezed herself in between Tobo and his father, is patting his face caressingly, saying, "Poor pappy, poor pappy, how hot he is!" A painter, who could have done justice to this group, would have produced a charming picture.

Mr. Paragreen, as may be inferred, is just come

in from an early walk, and is giving his children an account of what he has been able to achieve. First, he had been to Galignani's, and bought a capital map and Guide of Paris — so for the future no fear of their being led astray; then he had gone to the box-office of the Italian theatre, and, by almost miraculous good luck, found two tickets just brought back by a gentleman and lady suddenly telegraphed for from Brussels; finally, on his way home, he had chanced on a flower-market quite near the hotel, and bought for Ma that beautiful bouquet of moss roses lying on the table with the Guide. "And so, my dears, you must manage to amuse yourselves this evening as well as you can, while mamma and papa are at the play."

"Do they sing and dance at the Italian play, pa?" asks Emma.

"No, my dear, it's acting."

"Oh!" says Arabella, more advanced in worldly knowledge than Emma, "I thought Italian people always sung."

"That's at the Opera, you silly child," says Tobo.

"Quite true," says Mr. Paragreen, "but this evening it is to be acting, little Emma; and the people will speak to each other, as we all do, you know."

"Do they quarrel too, papa?"

"Sometimes, my dear. Well then, my poppets, as the play would not do for little folks, who would be sure to fall asleep: Da, like a dear girl, as she is, stays at home to take care of sisters, and Tobo stays to see that no one runs away with Da," pinching her blushing cheek; "and to-morrow, if we are all good, why, we'll go and dine — at Corazza's, in the Palais Royal."

The two little girls clapped their hands in delight; Ida looked pleased, and Tobo, whose countenance hitherto had been clouded over, brightened up. From the time the trip to Paris was decided on, Corazza had been a sort of promised land, to which the Paragreen family were one day to have access; and the imaginations of the younger members had ever since been busily at work in that direction. Corazza was the Parisian hobby-horse of Alderman Joliffe. "If you wish for a good dinner, old fellow," that magnate had said to Paragreen, "let Very and the Friars Prove and So alone, and you go to Corazza's."

At this moment Mrs. Paragreen joins the party, and is saluted by four merry voices, singing out together, "We are to go to Corazza's to-morrow, ma!" Mr. Paragreen rises, shakes himself free, and presents the moss roses, with a most gallant air, to his lady, saying, "This is for you, Dora dear, ain't they lovely?"

"Beautiful — and this for you," says the lady, giving her husband a hearty kiss.

"I have got a Guide and map, my dear, and a couple of tickets to see Ristori this evening — she plays her best part, Mirra — now, haven't I managed well?"

"Charmingly! but you always do, Sylvester, when you put your mind to a thing. Thank you, I am so pleased."

It is easy to read in the beaming countenance Mrs. Paragreen turns on Mr. Paragreen, that her incessant pecking at her husband is a mere constitutional tic, a gymnastic exercise, necessary to her health perhaps, but which, after all, does not interfere in the least with her affection. In this happy disposition of mind they go to breakfast, and then sally forth, bound for the Exhibition.

People may talk as they like about missing the gigantic proportions of the transept of the London Crystal Palace, as well as the stately leafy veterans of Hyde Park, humbled to a modest size by the Babel-like height of the glass dome above; still it cannot be denied, that this Paris Palace of Industry has a magical spell of its own, which holds fast all who pass its portals. Look at the *ensemble* from one of the Galleries, and then say if there be no temptation to cry aloud, "Upon my word, this is beautiful."

Such, indeed, was the feeling of the Paragreen family, on their first entrance into the Palace; and for some little time after, they fluttered about in a sort of enthusiastic bewilderment. When, however, they came to examine the contents in detail, they discovered no ends of deficiencies, and plenty to criticise — the task is so easy! — Nevertheless, they found more yet to admire; so much so, that Mr.

Paragreen did not once begin speechifying on the comparative merits of the two Exhibitions, but contented himself with repeatedly declaring that "it was a move in the right direction." As for the ladies, from Mrs. Paragreen down to her smallest facsimile, Emma, they were all sight, — devouring with their eyes those beautiful bracelets, and those lovely veils — and it was "Oh, Ma! look at this," — and "Ida, come here — did you ever see anything so like cobweb?" In the Lyons Silk Department, Mrs. and Miss Paragreen stood long transfixed before a doll as large as life, dressed in a ball-costume, which shewed how far and wide fashion can go — the two comparing notes, and scanning and studying the puppet's attire with the utmost gravity. Mr. Paragreen, at last, forced them away to the Stereoscopes, where he was in his full glory, explaining and descanting.

But the fullest measure of time — sixty minutes, without the deduction of a second, a delicious hour of enjoyment, was given to Giroux's toys, the mechanical baby, which called out papa and mamma, the bleating goat, the nibbling rabbit, and especially, and above all, the fiddle-playing monkey, the identical graceful creature, if we are not mistaken, which had such success with His Royal Highness Prince Albert, that he became its ever-to-be-envied possessor. Nor must we forget that most portentously capacious of French grenadiers, who, without so much as a "Fi fa fum," swallowed Russian soldiers *ad infinitum*, laying them with relish on his tongue, as if they had been so many sardines — a truly national contrivance, that ought to have secured to its inventor a great gold medal, at least, if the Jury had had a spark of patriotism in them.

The honours of the day were, however, for the Crown Jewels, those darling "Diagmongs," as Mrs. Paragreen always styled them, and to get more than one sight of which, the rush about them being tremendous, mother and daughter cheerfully sacrificed the swelling volume of their flounces and crinolines, which came out of the jostle beaten down, like ripe corn after a thunderstorm. The Diamans de la Couronne were, as every one may remember, the culminating point of attraction of the Exhibition — one more proof, if any were wanted, of that admirable and infallible instinct of the masses for what is truly grand, and noble, and beautiful.

Such the objects which principally attracted the notice of the fairer portion of our family, such the sights which afforded them the most unmitigated satisfaction. By this we do not mean to insinuate that those of the stronger sex were insensible to the same charms. By no means. Mr. Paragreen and Tobo enjoyed the silks, and velvets, and dolls, and diamonds, extremely; but they were not exclusively engrossed by them, both father and son having individual preferences of their own. Tobo, for instance, doted on cannons, rifles, revolvers, yataghans, and in general on all engines of destruction, explaining *con amore* their use and destination, and horrible effects, to his sisters. Mr. Paragreen's taste, to use his own words, was for "the useful and cheap, my dears, all that tends to the improvement of the working classes," and, consequently, down into his notebook went all the prices marked on cheap articles. He was even about to begin a philanthropic speech on this subject, but Mrs. Paragreen cut it short by saying —

"Yes, yes, Mr. Paragreen, we know what you mean, but it's too hot here for holding forth. Do let us go and seek for something to eat and drink, — I am ready to drop."

Off set our six pilgrims in search of a buffet, and after getting entangled among pianos and organs, all hard at work — losing themselves in alleys of meerschaum and amber — and getting bewildered in labyrinths of long-cloth and broad-cloth — they at length reached the precincts allotted to creature comforts. "How nice! — how refreshing! — what dear little tables" — and so they seat themselves.

"What shall we order?" asks Mr. Paragreen.

"As it is only once in a way, let us do the thing handsomely," returns Dora, in a queenly manner, "and finish off with ices."

They were not, however, so engrossed by their agreeable occupation, as to be insensible to a sudden swell and heave of the human sea rolling by, nor to the sudden crash and break of the living waves in one direction. "The Prince! the Prince!" cried voices far and near, and many of the pretty little tables were instantly deserted. Up jumped our friends at the sound—some with spoons, some with napkins—darting away, heads down, heels up, like mad bulls in a china shop, and pursued by a detachment of alarmed waiters.

"Where is he?" gasps Mrs. Paragreen, swinging her napkin violently.

"Here, Dora, here!" cries Mr. Paragreen; and in his precipitation, running against, and trampling, and crushing the tender toe of a French captain of Spahis, just from Africa. The agonised captain bolted forth the most tremendous oath imaginable, winding up with a "Sacre Bedouin, va!" and an angry scowl, which, to say the least, suggested the expediency of an apology. Now, not to have saved his life, could Mr. Paragreen in his flurry remember any French phrase to the purpose; however, with a simple bonhommie not to be withstood, he exclaimed, "Anglais — Allié, you know," nodding his little green-covered head. The effect was instantaneous. A smile made the military gentleman's moustache quiver, as he grumbled, that "ce n'était pas une raison;" but he was disarmed. This trifling incident, which would not have graced these pages but that it gives another illustration of our hero's presence of mind under difficulties, did not prevent him and his party from being one of the foremost on the passage of Prince Napoleon, and receiving in return for their bows and courtesies the coveted nod, which made them delighted with him, and with everybody, and everything belonging to His Imperial Highness, white bournous included.

But this was only a foretaste of the pleasures in store for our family on this auspicious day; for no sooner had they emerged from the Palace into the Champs Elysées, on their way to the Flower Show, (after having honestly returned spoons and napkins, and settled the bill for the luncheon,) than they perceived at a glance, by the thick double row of people, and carriages lining each side of the avenue, that some great sight was at hand. What had been conjecture was made certainty by a smartly-dressed young man, whose light moustaches and tuft had been already recognised in the distance by one of the Paragreens' party. By chance or design this person reaching Mrs. Paragreen's side, took upon himself to appease her curiosity by imparting the information, that their Majesties were expected to pass almost directly on their way to the Tuileries. In such moments of thrilling expectation even a Joliffe of Hackney, you know, may waive all etiquette, and allow herself to be addressed by a stranger. Besides, he was such a perfect gentleman, observed Mrs. Dora, afterwards — so very useful, and obliging, getting chairs for them to stand on, helping the children up so kindly. Here Ida blushes like the rosiest of Auroras — who knows? — perhaps her pendant hand had received some little tender touch, which mamma knew nothing about. Mrs. Paragreen surmises that he is a person of quality.

By and bye their Majesties appear, and the Paragreens are in an ecstasy — the ladies fluttering their handkerchiefs, while father and son hurrah themselves hoarse. The crowd is grinned at by a long retinue of lords and ladies-in-waiting, equerries, maids of honour, aides-de-camp, and ministers of state; these last manipulators of the European olla-podrida being easily distinguished from the rest by a broader grin on their faces, which seems to say, "With what sauce would you like to be served up, good folks, eh?"

CHAPTER VII.

More Treats.

"Now, then," cries Mr. Paragreen, as a last huge cloud of dust, raised by the Imperial horses, hid the godlike pageant from vulgar eyes, "Now then for it." But this was sooner said than done.

Imagine Fleet Street, or London Bridge, only much larger, during the busiest hours of day, ploughed in all directions by omnibus, private carriage, hackney coach, cab, cart, grooms with led horses, and dandies on hired horses — all tearing this way and that, with that extreme care and regard for pedestrians which characterizes riders and drivers of all countries — in this respect Paris has nothing to envy London — and say, whether to get to the Flower Show on the other side of this crowded carriageway of the Champs Elysées, was not fraught with some danger to our worthy hero, his wife, and four children. Mr. Paragreen, nothing daunted, with that instinct for strategy which distinguished him, bade the family form in single file, Tobo at the head, the little girls in the centre, himself closing the line.

In this order they attempted the passage several times, but were always beaten back in disorder. The worst of the business was, that in the last advance Tobo, with the rash thoughtlessness of his youth, gave the company the slip, and with more than one narrow escape of being cut in two, or crushed to atoms, reached the opposite shore unharmed, and stood beckoning to the others to come over — as if it were not an affair of life and death.

A new attempt was foiled as the others had been. Mrs. Paragreen grew hot and angry, Emma and Arabella became frightened and stupid, and Mr. Paragreen was ready to tear his hair, when a voice close by was heard exclaiming — "Est-ce bien vous, Milord?" At this fascinating sound, Mr. Paragreen raised his eyes to see the happy mortal so addressed, and in so doing met the sparkling black eyes of — guess, imaginative reader — why, of His Highness the Prince of Something, Somewhere; who, on the driving-box of a beautiful britzka, with the reins of a beautiful pair of horses in his princely hands, was bowing to him in the most condescending manner possible. Could the Prince have called him — Mr. Paragreen, Milord? There could not be the slightest vestige of a doubt he had; for His Highness was impatiently dismissing a person standing on a front wheel of the carriage, with one hand on the splash-board, and the other on the Prince's arm, and who had very much the look of detaining the august driver against his wish.

His Highness hands the reins to one of the two well-got-up footmen in the back seat, whispers his obtrusive friend, pushes him aside, and nimbly jumps down on the pavement. "How are you to-day, Madame? — seen their Majesties pass, of course — looking fatigued — found your cards — thank you — never return visits, Mr. Pappagreen — I could not — I have no time, you understand."

The persons so addressed were overwhelmed by this condescension, and quite ready to drop on their knees. Mrs. Paragreen was twitching her head about to see if the standers by were remarking them.

"Do you know the gentleman who was speaking to me? The Prefect of the Seine — the same as your Lord Mayor. A good-hearted fellow, though rather troublesome: offers to make me gain fabulous sums — only five thousand down with a certainty of the gain of a million. A golden opportunity for men of capital like you, Mr. Pappagreen. I am a Prince without a capital — ha! ha! you take me. I have learned, you see, to joke about my misfortunes."

Here His Highness met glances of the sincerest and most admiring sympathy.

"But my sorrows have taught me another lesson, — to feel for others. You might have heard me begging of the Prefect — yes — I am always begging — quite a beggar. Ha, ha!"

The Paragreens receive this statement with a chorus of ohs! and ahs!

"I have a family — understand me — not my own — your country-folks — most excellent, respectable people, I assure you — once kept their carriage — sad reverse of fortune — reduced to a few hundred a year — almost to beggary — a most affecting case. Well — I have set on foot a sort of subscription for them — wish to Heaven I could do it all myself, but I must be patient! Now, Mr. Pappagreen — now, dear lady, will you not assist another charming father and mother?"

The Paragreens will be only too happy to contribute their mite.

"Ah! I knew you would — English hearts never appealed to in vain. Can I be of any use? where are you going? — to the Flower Show? — afraid to cross, my little maid (chucking Emma's chin)? Shall I take you over in the carriage?"

The Paragreens, in a tumult of emotion, fear to intrude. His Highness insists, lifts the children himself into the carriage, then assists in Mrs. and Miss Paragreen, and springs in after them, beckoning Mr. Paragreen to follow his example. The whole fry are ready to jump out of their skins for joy. Nothing is wanting to the perfect bliss of our excellent couple, but that Mrs. Jones should see them in their glory, and the word "Prince" emblazoned in letters of fire on His Highness's back.

"A great fête at Versailles to-morrow," says the Prince.

"Scarcely necessary to ask if His Highness is going," simpers innocent Dora.

"Of course he is," intimates the high Potentate, with a grave bend of the head, — "he must."

They are almost at the Flower Show — such an opportunity may never present itself again. "Now or never," thinks Mrs. Paragreen to herself, and then exclaims passionately — "Oh, dear! how I do envy your Highness, — what wouldn't I give to get a ticket!"

"Really, now — it would make you so happy!" replies the Prince, with a compassionate benignity. — "I am afraid it is next to impossible — the tickets must be all distributed by this time."

Even if they are, Mrs. Paragreen firmly believes if His Highness would only say a word, one word for them, — who could refuse His Highness? Really, the speaking face of our Dora of Peckham, at this instant, beats Ristori's for expression. His Highness silently acknowledges the potency of her look, and the cogency of her argument; for he meditates — then says, while helping the lady to alight —

"We shall try, Madam, at all events; if we do not succeed in this, we may for something else as good. Perhaps, Mr. Pappagreen, you would not mind talking the matter over with my Secretary — he knows better than I do myself what I can or cannot do. — By the bye, I dine at Prince Jerome's to-day, and probably I shall meet the Great Chamberlain. But really I must leave you. — Good-bye;" and he raises his hat as gravely as any crowned head could do. Then Jupiter, followed by six pairs of wondering eyes, the two belonging to the recovered Tobo included, climbs up to his lofty seat, seizes the reins with one hand, waves his whip with the other, and disappears in a cloud of dust, in the direction of — Olympus, perhaps. The Paragreens step into the garden, Mrs. Paragreen leading the way with the carriage of a queen.

"I say, Sylvester, what do you think of my little rooz day gare?"

"In fact, my dear, I was quite wonderstruck at

your" — impudence was on the tip of his tongue, but he changed it in time to — "presence of mind."

"Now confess, dear boy, that but for your wife you would never have had a chance of being as good as at court."

"Better not count our chickens till they are hatched, my dear," observed "dear boy" sententiously.

"What is the use of throwing cold water on things, Mr. Paragreen? if you had a spark of proper pride about you, you wouldn't speak in that way."

Mr. Paragreen bobbed his head down into a great bush of azaleas, which Ida called him to look at. "Are they not beautiful, mamma?"

"Very pretty indeed, my dear," says mamma, who glances at them with the greatest indifference. When a lady has been escorted in the great avenue of the Champs Elysées by a live prince in his own princely carriage — and there is a chance of her being at the same ball with an Emperor, an Empress, a Queen, and Highnesses uncountable, where is the azalea or rhododendron that is worthy of a thought?

When Mr. Paragreen's head emerged from the yellow azalea, he suddenly said —

"What could have made His Highness call me Milord?"

"Lor! Mr. Paragreen, you forget that he lives among the nobility — no wonder he makes such mistakes sometimes."

"Well, my dear, not knowing, can't say. By the bye, what are we to do about this subscription? I suppose two pounds is enough."

"I should say not," returned Dora, in her most resolute manner; "it is not every day we have to do with princes — give ten guineas, it's more genteel."

"Bless my heart! my dear, how fast you go! ten guineas! — no, no — that's paying rather too dear for the honour. I'll give five between us, and not another farthing!"

This point settled, husband and wife hastened after Ida and her sisters, who were fluttering like butterflies from one sweet flower to another — looking more natural and happy than they had done since leaving Eden Villa. Even Tobo condescended to admire the collection of fruits.

Mrs. Paragreen could not, however, be interested for more than a minute by anything she saw; and, resuming her interrupted chain of thoughts, she turned to Mr. Paragreen, saying —

"One thing I am determined on, — if I meet our precious ambassador at Versailles, I'll give him a lesson he won't forget as long as he lives."

"But, Dora, dear, we only left our cards at the Embassy yesterday morning, and —"

"I knew beforehand you would take his part against me, — no matter what it is, I am always in the wrong. What on earth are all those people staring at us for? I'd ask the great big boobies, if I could speak their horrid gibberish."

Mrs. Paragreen was quite justified in being astonished. Our family seemed to possess a greater magnetic attraction for most of the loungers in the garden, than the flowers they had come to see. Accustomed to attract a certain amount of notice wherever they went, they had at first paid no attention to the sensation they produced; but it gradually attained such proportions as to embarrass even them. If they walked, a procession walked in their wake — if they stood still, the procession stood still, and stared at them. The predominant feeling of the crowd seemed to be that of simple curiosity, so much so that Mrs. Paragreen observed, "Well, I never — I am sure if you were an hippopotamus, Mr. Paragreen, the people could not stare at you more."

"I can't think what it can be!," exclaimed Mr. Paragreen, looking anxiously at as much of his person as he could see. "Tobo, is there anything on my back?"

They received unaccountable looks of sympathy, also, and as unaccountable tokens of deference; for instance, a free passage was always left for the family, and many of the male spectators lifted their hats to them. Mr. Paragreen was so worried by having constantly to snatch at the limp brim of his little green covering, which he never could pull off in time — raising it was out of the question — that he had a momentary wild thought of carrying it in his hand, and going bareheaded; but he had a vague fear of being taken up as an impostor, — he therefore tried to find the gate by which they had entered.

Ere reaching it, two gentlemen, one of them an

officer, came up, and, after bowing, the one in plain clothes made a short speech, of which the only words Mr. Paragreen could catch, were "honneur," and "votre Seigneurie." It became at last evident to the Paragreens that they were mistaken for some one else; the little man, at his wit's end, bowed and better bowed, stammering forth a profusion of "pardongs" and "mercis." Then suddenly remembering the effect of the words, "Alliés — Anglais," on the captain of Spahis, he sung out — "Alliés, Anglais — Anglais, Alliés — hurra!" in his loudest voice. On this, some faint disjointed cheers arose in the crowd, and three voices were distinctly heard to cry — "Vivent les Anglais!"

Escorted by the civil gentleman in plain clothes, and the one in uniform, the Paragreens, half elated, half alarmed, were paraded through the garden, and at the gate had to swallow another oration, to which this time the exhausted Mr. Paragreen could only reply by a bow to every second word. Clapping his green hat firmly on his head after the last round of salem-aleks, as if there it should stick let what would happen — our hero shut his eyes, and dashed headlong through the open wicket, right into the midst of the throng there assembled — a throng so thick, that the sergens de ville on duty at the Flower Show had to use main force, to procure free egress for the family, and to protect their retreat.

Now, says the reader, with not a little pleasant malice, — how is the story-teller going to account satisfactorily for this ridiculous *qui pro quo?*

By the unvarnished truth. You remember His Highness calling Mr. Paragreen "Milord," a short while ago? Well, His Highness had his own reasons for so doing. You remember, also, that there was a person with a foot on the wheel of the princely carriage, and a hand on the splash-board of the same? Mr. Paragreen and his fair partner might be cheated into supposing the Prefect of the Seine, during Her Britannic Majesty's visit, had leisure to converse in such a delightfully convenient attitude, but the reader knows better than to believe His Highness's cock-and-a-bull story. The fact is, that even Highnesses have human weaknesses and human troubles, and that our Prince, to escape from the boring of a most pertinacious dun, had with monstrous courage and ability pleaded, and successfully pleaded, the propinquity of his friend, the Lord Mayor of London, incog., but not the less to be respected and revered. The disappointed creditor having gone also to the Flower Show, had pointed out Mr. Paragreen to one or two people as the Lord Mayor of London, come over incog. in Her Britannic Majesty's suite; the intelligence had spread like wild-fire, and quickly reached a Member of the Floral Committee, then in the garden, who, calling on the only person in authority at hand — viz., the officer on guard, had both of them —— but you know the rest. Is not this clear, simple, and natural, as truth always is?

Yes, but why did the Prince turn his dun into a Prefect?

Ah! since everything must be explained, is it not possible that he thought the mention of the Prefect of the Seine a better introduction to that little affair of the subscription, than either the mention of you or me?

CHAPTER VIII.

The Escapade.

THE table d'hôte was rather dull. It was perceptible at a glance that the ruling spirit of the company, its soul, as it were, was missing. But the conversation, which had flagged at first, acquired some briskness when Mr. and Mrs. Paragreen whispered to their immediate neighbours, who repeated it to theirs, and so on till the news had attained the widest circulation — that His Highness was that day to dine with Prince Jerome.

The intelligence was startling, coming as it did from the very lowest of the Lower Endians, and occasioned a good deal of cross-questioning, met by sharp and scornful retorts from Mrs. Paragreen, who said, "she supposed she knew what she was saying, having had the fact from the very own lips of His Highness, when they were taking a drive with him in his own britzka, in the Champs Elysées."

Glances of wonder and of envy shot hostilely towards the undaunted Dora, but no one ventured on any open defiance; observations critical and bitter circulated as to the absence of the shy gentleman; and the fat literary lady was peculiarly caustic, putting the question to the ceiling, "Whether certain persons should or should not be allowed admission into certain circles?" Mr. Paragreen fell into reveries, as to why the Prince had called him Milord. Mrs. Paragreen on the contrary was extremely on the alert, and out of all patience into the bargain, at the airs the Honorable A. Smallwhey was giving himself, and his patronizing speeches, as if he were the Prince himself. The cookery, however, was excellent, and that was some comfort.

As soon as the company rose from table, — much earlier than usual, as was natural in the circumstances, — Mr. Paragreen went up to His Highness's secretary, and begging his attention for a moment, repeated the conversation he had had with the Prince that morning, "by whose express desire," concluded our hero, "I seek an interview with you."

"Very good," said the functionary; "I am at

your service: may I beg of you to come to my bureau?"

Upon which our couple, dismissing the young ones to the attic, followed the secretary to a snug little room on the first floor, which had a combined air of elegance and of business about it.

The Prince's private secretary was a handsome, intelligent-looking man of thirty, speaking English fluently, and whose high-bred manners attested a familiarity with the best society.

"Pray be seated," and he placed himself at his own desk. "Now, Sir, will you kindly favour me with your name? — Sylvester Pappagreen?"

"Paragreen, Paragreen, Sir," protested the owner of that name.

"I beg pardon — no title? — Esquire? — Sylvester Paragreen, Esquire, of Eden Villa, Peckham. And you, Madam? — Mrs. Theodora Paragreen — one of the Joliffes of Hackney, you say? Ah! indeed! Now, then, the name of the person who presented you at Court — at the Court of St. James, I mean."

The husband and wife are struck dumb. Mr. Paragreen strokes his nose violently.

"Dear me," cries Mrs. Paragreen, recovering her speech, "must you have that?"

"Indeed I must, it is indispensable," returns the Secretary; "at least" —

"How awkward!" sighs the lady. "To tell you the truth, Sir, we have not been presented at Court yet; but my cousin, Alderman Joliffe, has."

"When I say indispensable," resumes the Secretary, "I mean with reference to admission, according to rule — by the grand entrance; but there is the back-door" — laying a great stress on the word.

"Is there?" cries the lady eagerly.

"Which opens with a golden key," winds up the man in black.

"With a golden key!!" repeated Mr. Paragreen.

"Yes, with a golden key," returned the imperturbable Secretary. "I take it for granted, that you would not think much of a twenty-pound note or so."

"Certainly not," said Mrs. Paragreen, with sharp decision.

"Twenty pounds!" exclaimed Mr. Paragreen; "pray, sir, may I ask what for?"

"For smoothing away little difficulties — with the Great Chamberlain," replied the Secretary, winking and smiling significantly.

"I understand," said the wife, brightening up.

"I don't understand," cried the husband, growing gloomy.

The gentleman in black rose, went up to Mr. Paragreen, laid his hand on the little man's sleeve, and said in a whisper — "You have no idea, sir, of the extent of" — (lowering his voice still more) — "of the extent of corruption in this unhappy country."

"You don't say so!" exclaimed Mr. Paragreen, his small eyes dilating with unfeigned astonishment.

"It is awful, sir, I assure you — this, of course, is quite under the rose — even the most exalted regions are not free from the taint. Do you take me now, sir?"

"I do, I do," sighed Mr. Paragreen; "but His Highness mentioned nothing of the sort."

"Of that I am sure — he would not for the world

— it would be utterly foreign to his character. He is too good, can never learn to say 'No' to any one — and what is the consequence? — that he squanders money right and left, and cannot command 5000 pounds, when that sum would command a fortune. His couple of thousand per month is a mere nothing for a man in his station of life, and it melts, sir, melts away. But, for God's sake! not a word on this subject to His Highness, or I shall lose my place."

"Oh!" ejaculated both the Paragreens simultaneously.

"Only yesterday," pursued the accomplished gentleman, "one of the finest horses in His Highness's stables went — to Somebody else's. Actual money never, but the equivalent *always* — appearances must be kept up, you know. For instance, His Highness goes to — never mind names — and says, 'There are two dear friends of mine (as in your case, perhaps) for whom I want invitations for the ball at Versailles — be a good fellow now, and shut one eye to any flaws in the title.' Well, the person so addressed says, 'Let them come under your wing, Highness, and I will be utterly blind, I promise you.' — Well and good. Now mark what follows. This person calls the next day, or the one after, and says, 'By the bye, Prince, I am come to ask where I could procure a few dozen of that same splendid Johannisberg you gave us at your last dinner.' The Prince of course takes the hint, and immediately sends four dozen of his Johannisberg — molten gold, I call it — and this is the way the best and kindest of Princes gets himself into difficulties."

All this was said so fluently, earnestly, and feelingly, that it elicited the warmest sympathy from our friends.

"Excuse my emotion," continued this phœnix of secretaries, his fine eyes brimful of tears, "my heart is overflowing, and I but discharge a duty. I know I am speaking to persons of birth, of fortune, and of feeling, and who would not, for anything this world could offer, take advantage of that which, I hope, I am not disrespectful in denominating His Highness's noble foible."

"Oh! never, never!" protested Mrs. Paragreen passionately.

"Of that you may rest assured," chimed in Mr. Paragreen, with dignity.

"Well, then!" said the Secretary, rising, "all that remains for me to say is, that I shall endeavour to ascertain the amount of the sacrifice imposed on His Highness on this occasion, and take the liberty of respectfully communicating it to you — that is, if you allow me to do so."

Mr. and Mrs. Paragreen unanimously agreed to this.

"Thank you — I need not add another word. This way, if you please — I rely on your profound secrecy. I shall take His Highness's orders, of course, and to-morrow morning will do myself the honour of calling on you early, to report progress. Will half-past nine suit you? — very good. Your most obedient servant."

Our pair from Peckham had been so impressed by the Secretary's eloquence, that, when a waiter stopped them on the stairs, to say that a carriage was at the door of the Hotel waiting for them, they had some difficulty in recollecting that they had bespoken one, and also for what purpose. They hurried to their rooms to give a few parting recommendations to Ida and Tobo, and then set off for the Italian Theatre.

Five minutes afterwards Tobo drew Da to one of the windows. "I say, Da," he began, "you don't mean really to stay moping here all the evening, with these two little brats, do you?"

"Certainly I do," replied dutiful Ida.

"Then you'll have to do it by yourself — for, I promise you, I won't. Come — don't be silly — put them to bed, and let's go out." The truth must be told, that Tobo wanted an accomplice.

"They will never go to bed at this hour, I am sure. It's broad daylight."

"Well, if it is, then we shall just have time for a turn in the Lizzies before dark — only a little turn, and we can be back before their bed-time."

"But they will be afraid to stay here without us."

"Nonsense. — Look here, Bella — you and Emma won't be frightened if Da and I go out for something — we shan't be long."

The children said they shouldn't be at all frightened; so Tobo clapped his cap on his head, saying, "Look sharp, Ida."

Still Ida hung back reluctantly. What would Pa and Ma say if they were to find out that they had left the children alone?

Tobo shrugged his shoulders, exclaiming, as he moved towards the door, — "Do as you like, Miss, I shan't ask you any more."

Ida was not proof against the temptation — she put on her bonnet, giving, as an excuse to herself for yielding, her wish to prevent Tobo from staying out too late.

Five minutes after, brother and sister, arm-in-arm, were strolling up the principal avenue of the Champs Elysées.

The tasting alone of the forbidden fruit was a treat — it was charming to move about in perfect freedom, to stop and enjoy what was to be seen, or go on wherever fancy led them. But Tobo's energies yearned for some better employment than this. The "Café Chantant des Ambassadeurs," all in a blaze of coloured lamps, proved ultra-alluring; and he had the courage to propose to his sister, that they should venture within the rope, and sit down at a little table, and ask for a glass of something. But to this Ida could in no way be persuaded, upon which Tobo called her a deceitful monkey, who was good for nothing but to spoil sport, and threatened to go in himself, and leave her outside. "Oh! I daren't, Tobo — you know ladies oughtn't to go to cafés, but I'll do anything else you like."

With this understanding they walked on without stopping, till they came to Guignolet's Theatre, just at that interesting crisis when Guignolet, a near relation of Punch, armed with a powerful staff, knocks down, again and again, and for ever, the whole *dramatis personæ* — a moral piece of fun which never fails to elicit roars of laughter from crowded audiences of children, who, it is consoling to think, will be men and women in due time. Ida would fain have dallied here a little while; but Tobo, spurning the notion as childish, went on to a magnificent round-about in full activity. Here this great hobbledehoy insisted on Ida fulfilling her promise, and, in less time than it takes to say it, brother and sister were whirling round, he on one of the wooden horses, she in a boat.

Tobo performed marvels, in the way of thrusting his mimic lance through the rings, and bearing one off at each turn — and, as surely as he did so, having his vanity tickled by the murmurs of approbation from the bystanders, one of whom, especially, was very loud in the boy's praise. "Bravo! well done! England against the field — Bravo!" In the heat of action, and in the excitement of success, Tobo had not observed from whom proceeded these enthusiastic plaudits; but Ida, less delighted with her position, had perceived, from the very first, that they came from the owner of the identical light tuft to the chin — from that particular *he*, we mean — whose expressive pantomime had already, more than once, made her aware of his ardent admiration for her; and who, at this present moment, while applauding the brother, discharged the most passionate glances at the sister.

When Tobo, having had enough of the fun, went to help his sister out of the boat, he found already in the discharge of that duty a dashing young man, who warmly congratulated the young Peckhamite, and asked, as a favour, to shake the hand which could accomplish such clever deeds. The boy at once recognised, in the speaker, the stranger who had been so obliging to the whole squad in that morning's crowd, and considering him, therefore, as something of an acquaintance, had no objection to be shaken hands with and complimented. This led to a little further conversation, in the course of which Tobo, having complained that he was as thirsty as if he had swallowed all the dust of the Lizzies, the three walked away together to a stand close by, where iced lemonade was sold.

"I must have something to warm this confounded cold stuff," said the would be-man in turndown shirt collars, and the something came in the shape of a rich golden-coloured liquor, yclept brandy. The harum-scarum young fellow poured a large dose of this into his lemonade, and drained it off at a draught, to the grief and terror of Ida, who faintly cried, "Pray don't."

This pathetic "don't" called forth an indignant inquiry from Tobo, of whether she thought a drop of brandy was enough to floor him — and then he called bravely for more lemonade and more brandy.

While Tobo was disposing of his mixture, the stranger, as in duty bound, was making the agreeable with all his might to Ida. How did she like Paris? She liked it very much indeed. Was her stay in Paris to be of any length? Ida was not sure, but she thought they would not remain more than another week or so. This intelligence was received with a deep sigh, and an exclamation of "What a pity!" that spoke volumes.

"Transporting place this Champs Elysées — isn't it?" This remark was addressed to Tobo, who, having done with his glass, was looking about him.

"Oh, yes! — it's well enough in its way — but don't come up to the Drive by the Serpentine — nothing to equal that in Paris."

"Ah! but you forget the Bois de Boulogne — why, it's like fairy-land, with its lakes, cascades, grottos, chalets, &c., and such lovely boats!"

"Where is this Boa de Bolone?" asked Tobo, "I never heard of it before."

"Not far on the other side of the Arc de l'Etoile — shall we go there now?"

Tobo looked willing, but did not answer directly.

"No, no!" cried poor Ida, "you know it is time we were at home."

Tobo felt degraded by this exposure.

"You may go home, if you like," he replied with manly dignity, "but as for me, I shall go to this Bois!"

"Oh, Tobo, do come home! what will pa and ma say?" The remonstrance was only adding fuel to the fire.

"It will only take us half an hour," expostulated the tempter, "see, there is my little brougham — allow me to drive you there — pray, say Yes."

"Yes, to be sure!" pronounced Tobo, moving decidedly towards the brougham pointed out.

What could poor Ida do, but follow her fractious brother into the carriage, and go with him and the unknown to the Bois de Boulogne?

The parents of the two runaways had, in the mean time, but little pleasure at the Italian Theatre. Neither of them had ever read Ovid's Metamorphoses, and they could not find out what Mirra was making herself so unhappy about. Mrs. Paragreen especially was out of all patience with such a silly daw of a thing, who didn't know what she wanted herself. Everybody so kind to her—father—mother—nurse —even that stupid what-d'ye-call-him in the armour —every one on their knees, praying and begging her for God's sake to say what was the matter with her, and she always crying, scolding, and complaining, and throwing up her eyes, and spreading out her hands like a maniac. Mrs. Paragreen knew what she would have done to this Miss Mirra, if she had been her daughter.

The drollest part of the affair was, that Mrs. Paragreen's dislike of the personage represented extended itself to the actress. In short, husband and wife were bored to death by the end of the second act, and agreed to beat a retreat. "This Ristori is quite the rage," observed Dora as they wended their way to the hotel, "so it's just as well to have seen her, for the sake of saying we have—but as for me, I declare I wouldn't give a fig for her acting."

"Nor I either," proclaimed Mr. Paragreen, "though,

perhaps, we mayn't have seen her in one of her best characters. It certainly was a dull affair."

"I wonder why all tragedies, and those other things — you know what I mean, must needs be so gloomy, and every one in them so miserable. A real bit of fun, that makes one like to die of laughing, there is some sense in that; but I should like to know where's the use or amusement of setting a parcel of people crying?"

Discussing such deep theories on Art, the senior Paragreens reached their hotel, and were lighted up to their rooms. "Mercy on us!" cried the lady, on arriving at the landing-place of the upper floor, "what can be the matter with the children? I hear them crying;" and rushing into the drawing-room, fancy the shock the parents received, when they beheld Emma and Arabella huddled up in one corner of the sofa, and weeping as if their little hearts were breaking.

"Where are Ida and Tobo?"

"They went out, ma, directly you and pa were gone; and when it got dark we were afraid, and couldn't help crying." Such was the doleful account sobbed out by the little girls.

"Gone out!" gasped forth husband and wife.

"Really, I must make an example of that boy," says Mr. Paragreen in an ominous voice; "he shall be made to hear reason, I am determined."

"And Ida!" exclaimed Mrs. Paragreen, "she's twenty times worse than Tobo; — boys will be boys — but that unfeeling girl" —

As the exasperated mother paused the door opened, and the two culprits made their appearance, Ida with a countenance giving the lie direct to her mother's apostrophe. Mrs. Paragreen crossed her arms and began.

"So this is the way a dutiful daughter replaces her absent mother, is it?"

"Oh, mamma!" implored Ida.

"This is the way, is it, a grown-up young lady takes care of her innocent little sisters, who, for anything she knew or cared, might have played with matches, set the house on fire, and burned themselves to death!"

"Oh, mamma!" entreated Ida.

"Have I nursed a viper in my bosom, have I?"

"Oh, mamma!"—Ida could stand it no longer, and threw herself at her mother's feet, sobbing convulsively.

"Where have you been, Sir?" asked Mr. Paragreen of the masculine offender, in a tone of a Rhadamanthus.

"To take a turn in the Lizzies," was the brief answer.

"Champs Elysées, Sir — that's how well-educated gentlemen speak," says the father sternly. "Precious short turn it has been! Do you know what o'clock it is, Sir?— a quarter to ten, Sir."

"How could I know? I have no watch," replied Tobo, rather sullenly.

"And it'll be long before you have one, Sir, if you go on behaving as you do; your conscience, Sir, ought to have stood in the place of a watch. Your behaviour, I regret to say, is a—ah!—is a—is most unbecoming. You ought—I am, I mean—yes, I am — positively ashamed of you. Don't speak — go to your room, Sir"—

This, to say the truth, was rather difficult to do,

for room Tobo had not, his night's repose being taken on the very sofa occupied at that moment by the two little girls and the majestic Mrs. Paragreen, with the still weeping Ida at her feet.

"Go to your bed, Sir, — I mean," went on Mr. Paragreen, rectifying his mistake, "and sleep if you can."

Having thus spoken, Mr. Paragreen took up a candle and walked towards an inner door, but after two steps he wheeled round, raised the hand with the candle in it, and slowly and solemnly let this awful sentence drop from his lips — "We don't go to Corazza's to-morrow," and disappeared. Mrs. and Miss Paragreen followed, leading Emma and Arabella, whose tears broke forth afresh at the terrible award, and Tobo was left alone to his sofa — and his remorse.

Ida remained long closeted with her mother that night; and the full confession she made was received in a spirit of truly motherly indulgence. Mrs. Paragreen went even so far as to assure her daughter that, if the person in question came forward honourably, and was well born and well off — in a word, such as could make her child happy, she, her mother, would raise no objections. "I should not much wonder, Ida, dear," concluded Mrs. Paragreen affectionately, "if he were to turn out to be somebody — a son, or grandson, or nephew of a nobleman, or baronet, or a Member of Parliament. Were there two horses to the carriage? — only one, but a very fine one, you say. Well, I believe most single men of rank only drive one horse till they get married. Good night, my dearest girl, and pleasant dreams to you."

Mrs. Paragreen had a pleasant dream herself. She dreamed that she was figuring in a quadrille at Versailles with His Imperial Majesty for a vis-à-vis, and that His Majesty asked her if she had anything or anybody to complain of, and that she answered—only of the British Ambassador, who had slighted her. On hearing this, His Majesty had ordered the culprit to be forthwith summoned to his presence, and beheaded on the spot. Mrs. Paragreen, prostrating herself however at His Majesty's feet, had, though with some difficulty, obtained the criminal's pardon; and turning to His Excellency had said — This is the way a Joliffe of Hackney revenges HERSELF!!!

CHAPTER IX.

Highly Confidential.

NEXT morning, at half-past nine, His Highness' secretary entered the little drawing-room in the upper regions of the Unicorn Hotel, where the Paragreen family were assembled, waiting for him — the seniors seated in state on the rather faded yellow sofa, which poor Tobo had been called upon to abandon much earlier than usual, to give the waiter time to make all circumstantial evidence of sheets and blankets disappear.

"Good morning, Mr. Pappagreen — beg pardon — Paragreen — delighted to see you so well, Madam — how are these charming little creatures?"

"You are very kind — quite well — I thank you — pray, be seated, Sir — Ida!" here Mrs. Paragreen nods to her eldest daughter, with a most significant side look at Emma and Arabella. Obedient Ida takes the hint, and prepares to leave the room with the children.

"Not on my account, I beg," interposes the polite visitor, "do not deprive me of the sight of any of your beautiful family. It is really not necessary — I dote on children, I assure you I do," stooping and embracing the two little girls quite fondly. "His Highness sends his compliments, (this to the father and mother of course,) and begs you will be ready precisely by eight o'clock this evening, to go — you know where," (with a wink.)

"How very k—"

"His Highness will take you in his own carriage. He dines in his apartment to-day, and will send to let you know when he is ready."

"How very kind of His Highness!" exclaim Mr. and Mrs. Paragreen, in raptures.

"I mention no place, as it is His Highness' express desire, that the whole thing be kept secret, especially from any of the people in the house. You understand the Prince's reasons — wishes to excite no jealousies — cannot do for every one that comes in his way, what he is happy to do for his friends."

The Paragreens understand the Prince's reasons perfectly, and will be as silent as tombs.

"Are you an admirer of cameos?" the query is put to Mrs. Paragreen, who, rather startled by it, replies, "Yes — that is — not particularly — I don't like the great bunches on their backs."

The Secretary, startled in his turn, "Ha! I see — I don't mean camels, but cameos — rare stones worked *in relievo*. I thought you might perhaps like to see one, reckoned a *chef-d'œuvre*, so I brought it with me — here it is;" and producing a small casket, the considerate gentleman displays to the admiring eyes of all the family a large brooch. Mr. Paragreen looks at it, Mrs. Paragreen examines it, Tobo, Ida, and the children are shown it, and each in turn pronounces it "beautiful."

"Is it not? — the subject, you see, Leda and the Swan — the Swan is Jupiter, as you know. His Highness got it at Rome from Bianchini, the famous lapidary — had it too for a mere trifle — guess how much?"

Mrs. Paragreen has not an idea, Mr. Paragreen ventures to suppose a couple of pounds or so.

"Oh, Sir! — a stone 2000 years old, and of such workmanship, two pounds! — you must be joking.

Why, His Highness, when he paid down 125 scudi for it, considered he had got a great bargain. See, here's Bianchini's own receipt for that sum, — 125 scudi Romani, that is, in English money, twenty-five pounds, neither less nor more, (the exact amount of the sum, I promised to communicate.)"

These last words were whispered in a stage *aparté*, intended for Mr. and Mrs. Paragreen's ears alone, and acknowledged by affirmative nods of intelligence from both those wise heads.

"And," resumes the speaker, "this cameo I am commissioned to convey as a gift from His Highness to — better to name no names — to a person of high standing at Court, who, only yesterday, had an opportunity of obliging His Highness in an affair which His Highness had much at heart — much at heart."

Every syllable of this last phrase, underlined by the accent of the speaker and by the winks with which it was accompanied, was responded to by an equally expressive pantomime from the husband and wife, intimating clearly to the orator that his picturesque style of colouring was not lost upon them.

The secretary now rose to depart. — "By the bye, how stupid I am, I was about to forget — His Highness, though, was so particular in his instructions — that business of the subscription. His Highness spoke to you of it, I believe — yes, yes, certainly. Here's the list of subscribers;" and, reseating himself, he drew from his pocket and unfolded a sheet of foolscap paper. "Their Imperial Majesties, Her Most Gracious Majesty of England, the Princess Mathilde, Prince Jerome, Her Highness the Grand Duchess of Baden, Count Walewski, the Earl of Clarendon, Viscount Palmerston, &c., &c. You see you will be in good company," remarked his secretaryship, smiling.

"Will you put us down for five guineas?" faltered Mrs. Paragreen; "it is but little" —

"Oh! my dear madam, no excuses. I know the proverb, 'Many a little makes a mickle.' Thank you. Do you wish to be put down separately, or — very good, together — thus, Mr. and Mrs. Paragreen of Eden Villa, Peckham, five guineas. Thank you. Shall we write down the names of the other members of your family at a guinea each? Not for the sake of the money so much as for the morality of the thing. It is so refreshing to see youth engaged in works of benevolence."

"Very refreshing, indeed, sir, very," stammered forth Mr. Paragreen, at a loss what to say, yet feeling the necessity of saying something in answer to the appeal of the interrogative black eye.

"As Ida is the eldest her name must come first," said Mrs. Paragreen.

"Quite so — Miss Paragreen, one guinea, Mr.?" — glancing at Tobo.

"Thomas," suggested the lad.

"Mr. Thomas Paragreen, a guinea."

"Miss Arabella," prompted the father, "ten shillings and sixpence. Some distinction ought to be made between the eldest and youngest."

"Very sensible observation. I had not thought of it, I confess — good! Then we are to say, Miss Arabella Paragreen ten shillings and sixpence, Miss Emma Paragreen ten shillings and sixpence. The names look uncommonly well grouped together, don't they? Now, let me see, five and two, seven, and one more, eight — eight guineas in all."

Mrs. Paragreen nudged her husband's elbow. Mr. Paragreen plunged his hand into the left-side breast-pocket of his coat, and produced a pocket-book. Mr. Paragreen, as a practical man, had, since he set off on his travels, adopted the plan of carrying all his money upon his person, but with the precaution of securing the book which contained it to the bottom of his pocket by means of a stout string, long enough to allow of its being conveniently handled when need were.

"Eight guineas, you say, that is eight pounds eight shillings," calculated Mr. Paragreen aloud, as he opened the valuable book, and exhibited to view a considerable amount of Bank of England notes.

"Yes, eight pounds eight shillings, to which, perhaps, it may be agreeable to you," insinuated the secretary, "to add the sum, the figure of which I had the honour to communicate confidentially."

"By all means!" said Mrs. Paragreen, swallowing the bait. Indeed, had she not done so, she must have been made of stone, so temptingly was the hook dressed.

"Since you will have it so, let it be so," continued the gentleman in black, with a bow of resignation. "Your little debt then will amount to — 25 and 8 makes 33 — just £33 eight shillings — can it be so much? — yes, I am right, — £33, 8s."

Mr. Paragreen, with a rather wry face, tendered £35 in three bank-notes, and received back 32 shillings in French money. This business transacted, the smiling glossy visitor patted Emma and Arabella on the head, and bowing his adieux to the rest, reiterated emphatically, "At eight o'clock precisely, remember," and took himself and the £33, 8s. most serenely away. After all, why not? perhaps he felt as if he had well earned it by all the pains and trouble he had taken.

"What an amiable young man," said Mrs. Paragreen, "and so clever!"

"Very clever!" emphasized her husband, rousing himself from a reverie, "very clever indeed! Come, let's have breakfast."

They went to breakfast accordingly, which over, Mr. Paragreen put the usual question to his wife, "What are we going to do to-day?"

"You are going to take the children with you,

and keep them away, too, as long as possible — that's your business for the day." Such were the summary directions given by the lady. "Ida will stay with me — I want her. Thanks to somebody, I'm obliged to be my own maid, you know."

Mr. Paragreen saw breakers ahead, and put out to sea at once, taking Tobo and the young ones in tow. They went first to the Hôtel de Ville, where a little mortification awaited our practical sight-seer. Having, among other things, desired the person who shewed the rooms to let them see the guillotine, Mr. Paragreen was asked in a resentful tone, how he came to suppose that such toys were kept for exhibition at the Hôtel de Ville, and whether he took him for the executioner. But Mr. Paragreen, though a little thrown back, did not fail to draw from his defeat food for an instructive lecture to his children.

"It is kept there, I am sure," said he as they came out, "I had my information from Joliffe, who saw it with his own eyes. They are probably ashamed to show it — it is to their credit if they are. Guillotining is a most barbarous mode of putting people to death: hanging is almost pleasant in comparison.

These French, it must be owned, are behind us in most things — very far behindhand indeed."

Having thus settled the matter, Mr. Paragreen and his party proceeded to the Jardin des Plantes — the real object of their walk in fact — where they met with neither mortification nor disappointment, to cloud their enthusiastic admiration. Every trace of their natural annoyance at missing a sight of the guillotine, was lost in the keen enjoyment of looking at elephants and giraffes, in wondering at the playfulness of the hippopotamus and his companion, and at the monkeys and snakes — in rambling about the well laid out grounds, and munching buns *ad libitum* in the cool shade of the spacious avenues.

In short, father and children were so delighted and engrossed by the pleasures of the present moment, that had they not, by a miraculous chance, met with an empty citadine to take them back to the hôtel, they could not have avoided being too late for dinner, this eventful day of all the days in the year.

CHAPTER X.

Between the Cup and the Lip.

Mrs. Paragreen was just emerging from the hands of a hair-dresser, with whom and his performance she was finding fault, as her husband and children came in. Mother and daughter had spent most of the day out of doors also, but occupied in purchases connected with the toilet for that evening; and Mrs. Paragreen had found cause to say at least twenty times to Ida, during their rambles, "I have to thank your father, my dear, for all this botheration."

One annoyance or another had developed in our fair friend a certain asperity of temper, which was not likely to be mended by the necessity of sitting very still and upright, for fear of deranging her head-dress, à la Pompadour, or by the ill-dissembled laughter and ridicule it evoked from the ladies at table, (did not the fat blonde, indeed, go so far as to ask Mrs. Paragreen, with ironical politeness, if she were going to the fête at Versailles?) not to mention a certain conversation which she could not help overhearing, and to which we may have to refer by and by.

By the time dinner was over, Mrs. Paragreen was in a downright rage, and poor Ida had to bear the brunt of it all, besides being lectured the whole time she was helping her mother to dress, on the duties of elder sisters in their mother's absence, in a manner she was not likely to forget very soon. Mr. Paragreen held his tongue, and kept as much aloof as he could. The last stroke of eight o'clock was still vibrating when the queer servant in the ambiguous dress appeared, to summon the two lucky mortals to the august presence of His Highness. Mrs. Paragreen was, of course, not ready; her fan was missing, and her bouquet-holder, most indispensable component parts of a lady's dress, as every reasonable person knows. They were found at last, and then Mr. and Mrs. Paragreen were ushered into the sanctuary.

His Highness, in the garb of a golden pheasant,

that is, glittering with gold from head to foot, and with ribbons and cordons round his neck enough to have hanged him twenty times over, was standing in that peculiar attitude which we see assigned to potentates figuring at the street-door of miniature painters and photographists, we mean, by the side of a diminutive table, covered with a crimson cloth, his left hand on the hilt of his sword, his right on a portfolio, bearing in rich embroidery his Prince's coronet and initials, lying on the table.

"Well, Mr. Pappagreen, not yet dressed?"

"Not dressed, your Highness?" faltered the little man, scarcely crediting his own ears, and adding mentally, — not dressed, a man in open-worked stockings, pumps, white cravat, white waistcoat, and diamond studs in the front of his shirt?

"Not in uniform, I mean," explained the Prince. "You must be in uniform this evening; it is quite indispensable, and so is a manteau de cour for your lady."

"A mantua de gure!" gasped forth the wife.

"A uniform!" stammered the husband; "a uniform of what?"

"Of the rank you hold in society," said the Prince. "Are you not an officer in the army, or navy, or militia, — a lieutenant of a county, a magistrate, sheriff, constable, in short, something or other?"

"I am only a churchwarden," replied Mr. Paragreen dejectedly.

"Capital! that's the very thing. Put on a churchwarden's uniform."

"But churchwardens have no uniform," objected Mr. Paragreen.

"Never mind — make one — a fancy uniform, whatever you please, and call it a churchwarden's. I cannot introduce you in plain clothes, the thing is impossible; and you, dear madam, pray, forthwith order a manteau de cour. I cannot say how much I feel for your disappointment. I am disappointed myself. But we will find a way some other time of making up for it."

And with this promise of empty air to feed upon, the poor Paragreens were dismissed.

"Upon my word," said Mrs. Paragreen, with a

dreadful smile, "you are worth your weight in gold, Mr. Paragreen."

"I?—what have I done now?"

"Whatever you have a hand in goes wrong. It was not necessary to be a genius to ask about what dress we ought to wear."

"I beg your pardon, my dear, but I never thought of it," said Mr. Paragreen, humbly. "I really cannot think of everything."

"You needn't tell me that. I found that out long ago, to my cost. God knows when such an opportunity as this may happen again — most likely never. However, I won't have the same thing occur twice; so to-morrow, the first thing we do, let us go and order a mantua de gure, and some sort of uniform for you."

"We'll think about it, my dear," returned the husband; adding in a most conciliatory voice, "We are spending lots of money, Dora, dear — we are indeed!"

"BRICKS and MORTAR!!" burst forth Mrs. Paragreen, turning sharply round upon him; "don't speak nonsense, man."

Mrs. Paragreen was wont to swear by BRICKS and
MORTAR, just as Jupiter did by the Styx, on grand
occasions. An experience of some date had taught
Mr. Paragreen, that when she said Bricks and Mortar, the wife of his bosom was ready to come to extremities, and his heart misgave him. He therefore
took advantage of Mrs. Paragreen's flouncing into
the inner room, to whisper to Ida that, if he were
wanted, he was gone to Galignani's to read the
papers, but would be back presently. And without
waiting for any reply, he bounced down stairs, made
straight for the livery stables close by, (a discovery
of the previous day,) and jumping into a cab, said
to the coachman, "Au Jardin d'Hiver."

Why to the Jardin d'Hiver? Just have the goodness to answer one question, or two, and you will
see. Were you going to be admitted some evening
for the first time to the presence of Emperors, Empresses, Queens, Prince Consorts, &c., do you think
you could preserve your every-day sedateness and
equanimity? Certainly not. You would feel considerably elated, excited, and flurried. And if, added
to this, you had the happiness of having by your

side an amiable wife in a state of exacerbation, don't you think that this circumstance would tend materially to heighten the effervescence of your spirits? Thank you for giving us an honest "Yes." We then may take it for granted, that Mr. Paragreen was in that state of nervous flutter, in which a man is scarcely aware of what he is doing, and it can therefore cause no wonder, if, mechanically and without knowing that he did so, he applied himself more frequently than usual at dinner to the wine bottle by his plate, and entirely overlooked what Tobo was about, who, up to this day, had never helped himself to wine, without the inevitable admonitory, "Now, Tobo," from his father.

It was during these dubious moments that the druggist's assistant, that "vulgar poisoner," as Mrs. Paragreen called him, took it into his head to begin extolling the Jardin d'Hiver as the most charming and diverting place in Paris. The Jardin d'Hiver? what went on there? was it balls or concerts? was there good company? — to all these queries the young scapegrace would vouchsafe no more explicit answers, than sputtering bursts of laughter, and in-

sidious — Go and see for yourself — with expressive
side-glances at the fairer moiety of the company —
and sundry kicks on Tobo's calves, the young
chemist's vis-à-vis.

This mystery, which, in ordinary circumstances,
would have left Mr. Paragreen's imagination at least
undisturbed, had, owing to the repeated potations of
father and son, an effect on both — neither of whom
left the table without asking where this bewitching
place was, and at what hour it opened. This was
the conversation alluded to a few pages back, as
contributing its drop to the amount of gall already
fermenting in Mrs. Paragreen's bosom, and which
drew from that lady, as they were going up stairs,
the "hope that Mr. Paragreen was sufficiently a
Christian, a gentleman, and a father, not to think of
debasing himself by a visit to such a den of perdition." Higher cares had diverted Mr. Paragreen's
thoughts from this channel, but when, after the
signal slip of the cup of bliss from his lip, he found
himself in full dress, and with nothing to do, and
Mrs. Dora rather dangerous of approach, he bethought him of the druggist's dinner conversation.

Mr. Paragreen then communed with himself, whether, as a practical man, he had not better use the hour or two so unexpectedly at his disposal, and see that reproduction of the gardens of Armida in the Champs Elysées. Such was the concatenation of circumstances which led Mr. Paragreen to that den of perdition of the Jardin d'Hiver.

He deserved what he found, and that was a soirée de concert — very orderly, very dull, very innocent — and very scantily attended; just what a deceived wife's heart could desire. Mr. Paragreen looked right, then left, seated himself in a comfortable corner, listened a while to the music — but ignorant whether it was German or Italian, knew not if he were to admire, or find it detestable — and finally fell asleep.

On hearing from Ida that Mr. Paragreen was gone out, his worthy spouse made no remark, but went to the window, and began a devil's tattoo on the glass. After half an hour of this agreeable exercise, Mrs. Paragreen started from her chair, saw the little girls to bed, put on her bonnet, desired Ida to get hers on, and went all the way to the Jardin d'Hiver without articulating a word. Her countenance was appalling as she entered those dreaded precincts — from her eyes darted flames, — indeed, with her red bonnet on, she might have sat for a Tisiphone.

However, she was no sooner able to take in at a glance the general physiognomy of the place, than its dulness told on her. It was like oil poured on surging waves — her contracted features relaxed — half a smile even played on her lips, at sight of the innocent culprit snoring placidly in his corner.

"What is the news in Galignani's Messenger? eh!"

At these words hissed in his ears, Mr. Paragreen sprung up, saw his wife, and began to tremble.

"To procure an innocent pleasure for a careful wife, money is wanting, but money can be found and squandered for a husband's dissipation!"

"Oh, Dora! twenty sous," expostulated Mr. Paragreen, with a comical mixture of fear and fun.

"Twenty sous is too much to pay for putting one's self in harm's way, Mr. Paragreen."

"In harm's way!" repeated Mr. Paragreen, with an appealing look all round the room.

"Now then, Mr. Paragreen, let us make an end of it. Are we to order this uniform and the mantua de gare, or *not?*"

"Well, my dear, if you insist on it, I suppose we must," was the subdued reply, "but really we are spending lots of money — upon my honour, we are — only this morning's work cost us £33, 8s., Dora, my love."

"We shall be as saving as you like afterwards, I promise you faithfully, Sylvester — but you must grant me this — call it a whim, or what you please, but let me have my way. Just think of Mrs. Jones — and how all Peckham will know, who has a right to take the lead."

"Certainly — but, Dora — the Queen goes away on Monday, and to-day is Thursday — are we to throw away our money for nothing?"

"Suppose the Queen does go, she doesn't take away the Emperor and the Empress, and their Court, or the Tuileries, or the kings who are coming, and all that, does she?" rapidly recapitulated Dora with a rising colour. "Besides, hasn't His Highness promised us? — you don't doubt his word, do you?"

"Well, my dear, you shall order what you like, I always try to let you have your own way — now, don't I?"

"That's speaking kindly and like yourself. — Take you all in all, I don't think there's a better husband to be found in Christendom. — We had better be going, though."

"Bless my heart!" exclaimed Mr. Paragreen, as he put up his glass half-way to the door. "I say, Dora, look there!"

And a trying sight it was for a mother. Tobo, supported by the "vulgar poisoner," was in the act of crossing the room — his face as white as the handkerchief he held to his mouth.

"What's the matter, Tobo?" cried father and mother, in great alarm.

"It's the confounded music," hiccuped poor Tobo, "such an effect upon me — oh! oh!"

The chemist, leaving his young friend in the care of his parents, ran to look for a coach, and being fortunate enough to find one, Tobo was lifted into it, and taken home. There he was immediately consigned to his bed, and had a plentiful supply of hot camomile, and coffee, thanks to which the equilibrium of his stomach was somewhat restored. The whole time, Tobo never ceased complaining of the music, that horrid French music, which had quite upset him

The music, it is needless to say, was not guilty. Tobo had made an appointment with his acquaintance, the young man of the drugs, to go together to the Jardin d'Hiver. They had taken, on their way thither, a moderate allowance of brandy and water, from which Tobo would have felt no ill effects at all, had he not in his foolish love of aping his elders, insisted on smoking a cigar, because the druggist did. The cigar made him feel deadly sick, but he concealed his sufferings, till the heat of the room rendered any further dissembling impossible.

The odour of tobacco exhaled by the lad's whole person, revealed to his father and mother the real nature of his attack; but their parental bosoms were full of compassion, so they put off all lecturing till the morrow.

CHAPTER XI.

Mysterious.

THE first thing Mr. and Mrs. Paragreen did on the morrow of that eventful evening was to go out in search of a uniform and manteau de cour, an undertaking not without its difficulty; for, having naturally gone to a tailor, in whose windows they saw, in monumental letters, "English spoken here," and to a dressmaker, with the same intimation on her brass-plate, our couple discovered what was quite as natural, that not a soul on either premises could speak an intelligible word of the coveted language.

Fortunately, both the talented artists applied to had uniforms, and manteaux de cour in course of execution — a circumstance that, combined with the few words of French possessed by the husband, and the intelligent pantomime of the wife, enabled our friends to make a choice, agree on prices, and fix as the time for the delivery of the articles the following Tuesday.

The whole transaction did the greatest honour to the hearts of Mr. and Mrs. Paragreen, who vied with each other in discretion and generosity; he insisting on her choosing a costlier material and richer embroidery than that she had first decided on, she urging him, with all her eloquence, to take, instead of the rather sober and comparatively cheap dress of a Member of the Institute, a gorgeous uniform, which turned out to be that of a Marshal of France.

This matter settled, they returned to the hotel, and met on their way up stairs His Highness's secretary, who stopped to condole with them, in the most feeling tone, on their last evening's disappointment, adding that he could not, and never should, forgive himself for his stupidity in not having warned them about their dress, though even then, he feared, it would have been too late; and he ended by assuring them that this untoward event had utterly marred the Prince's pleasure at the Versailles fête.

The Paragreens said that His Highness was only too good, and that they had just been to bespeak a uniform and manteau de cour. The gentleman in black highly approved of what they had done; the more so, as he knew there was to be a State reception at the Tuileries during the ensuing week, and *now* they would have no disappointment to fear. Upon which assurance husband and wife pursued their journey to their high quarters with feelings of unmixed gratification — Mr. Paragreen more especially, who, during every second of this interview, had been in mortal apprehension of some "confidential communication."

This complacent mood of the parents was attended by the happiest results for the children, and in particular for Tobo, who confessed to Ida that he had got up expecting "a good dressing" from the governor. Mr. Paragreen, after a previous consultation with his wife, proclaimed at breakfast a general amnesty, and announced that they should dine at Corazza's. Smiles and happy little remarks darted about the breakfast table like dancing sunbeams, and not the least pleased of the merry group was the forgiver himself.

It was nearly midday when the phalanx took the field *en route* for the Exhibition. Mrs. and Miss

Paragreen had occupied much more time than usual in their preparations for going out, and the development of circumference about them, when they issued forth, gave them the look of balloons bent on taking flight, rather than of earthly beings made to walk on two legs. This anomalous appearance was the fruit of that "palaver" held by mother and daughter, as you may remember, before a doll in full dress, exhibited in the Lyons department of the Palace of Industry. They had, on comparing notes, come to the conclusion that they were deficient in that comely swelling out which fashion dictated, and had supplied the deficiency by the acquisition of two "Jupes à la Malakoff," those charming and graceful appendages, so dear, and justly so, to the fair sex. But enough of this digression.

After a cursory survey of the great nave of the Palais de l'Industrie, Mrs. Paragreen, as a matter of course, led the way to the Rotunda, the great altar, at which she loved to offer her devotions, and the adoration of the diamonds commenced. Mr. Paragreen and Tobo paid their tribute of homage willingly once, but seeing that the worship was not only about to recommence, but likely to last some time, they agreed to rendezvous on the Estrade at four o'clock, and then father and son went their several ways, leaving the mother and daughters to go theirs.

During this separation, Mr. Paragreen had a small adventure, scarcely worthy of being so called, but which we have our reasons for recording. Mr. Paragreen had, as we know, a habit of asking the price of everything he saw, a mere abstract pursuit, for he was without any ulterior views as to purchasing. On this day, a counter on which English china was displayed, particularly attracting his attention, he began his inquiries, and among other articles, asked the cost of a handsome dinner service. It seems that he had done the same on his first visit to the Exhibition, as the person in charge recognised the querist. Either having private reasons of his own for being out of sorts, or else being naturally coarse and cross, the china merchant answered gruffly, "What's the use of telling you? you are not one to buy anything."

Mr. Paragreen, stung to the quick by the well-aimed shot, replied angrily, "How do you know that?

I can tell you, I have enough of Bank of England notes in this" (flourishing his famous pocket-book) "to pay for all the trumpery in your shop. Put that in your pipe now, and smoke it."

And Mr. Paragreen, snorting and puffing, strode away. Under the smart of wounded pride he forgot (alas! even the most practical of men cannot always be on their guard) that it was rather dangerous to show a well-stuffed pocket-book in a crowd, without even a proclamation that the stuffing was of Bank of England notes.

At the appointed time Mr. Paragreen and Tobo joined the rest of the family in the Rotunda. Mrs. Paragreen's first greeting of her husband was, "Have you got your pocket-book?" "All safe, my dear," was the reply.

"Are you quite sure?"

"Bless my heart! quite sure," producing it; "what made you doubt it?" Mrs. Paragreen's flurried look and words more than justified this question.

"I could lay anything," said Mrs. Paragreen, in explanation, "that this place is full of pickpockets. I have been pushed, and jostled, and poked at, and what not, in a — most extraordinary manner — to say the least of it."

This was whispered by Mrs. Paragreen to her husband at intervals, as the whole party, joining hands not to be separated by the undulations of the crowd, strove to force a passage through the principal outlet from the Rotunda. All at once a sharp sound, as if of silk forcibly rent, and a scream from Mrs. Paragreen, spread a general alarm.

"What's the matter, Dora, dear?" cried the agitated husband.

"My gown, my good eight guinea gown, torn to pieces!"

The author of the mischief, a short and rather shabby individual, was begging ten thousand pardons in French.

"He did it on purpose," cried Tobo; "I saw him do it with my own eyes."

"So did I," interposed a tall, grey-whiskered, commanding-looking gentleman, stepping forward, and resolutely drawing the arm of the offender within his own.

"Suivez-moi chez le Commissaire, Monsieur, and

you," (turning to Mr. and Mrs. Paragreen, and speaking English,) "have the goodness to accompany us to the Commissary of Police, to give your evidence."

"This man stuck to us all the time we were in the Rotunda," remarked Mrs. Paragreen.

"The greater reason for having him examined," said he of the grey whiskers; "we shall soon manage his business for him."

The culprit betrayed symptoms of the greatest confusion, though all the while protesting in French that it was an accident, and that he was innocent.

"Tant mieux pour vous, si vous l'êtes," said the commanding-looking gentleman, "this way if you please, gentlemen and ladies, — we must teach these French to respect the English — it is a duty we owe to our country."

Mr. Paragreen would have willingly dispensed with that duty in the present instance — not that he felt for the criminal, if criminal he were — on the contrary, but our friend did not at all relish the idea of going before a French magistrate, with the probable annoyance of having to give his evidence in French; but he silently submitted, and followed his conductor to the office of the Exhibition Commissary of Police.

The affair was quickly arranged. Mr. Commissary listened gravely to the account given him in French by the tall commanding-looking gentleman, received Tobo's corroborative statement, made of course in English, and then ordered the tearer of gowns away, guarded by two sergens de ville, to Heaven knows what awful chastisement. This settled, he most politely invited Mrs. Paragreen, and her eldest daughter, if she liked, to pass into an adjoining room, where they would find women to mend Mrs. Paragreen's dress. While this was being done, the commanding-looking gentleman had ten minutes' private conversation with Mr. Paragreen, in the course of which he managed to draw from the *ci-devant* cork-merchant his name, address, former calling, domicile, size of family, income, nay, his wife's relationship to Alderman Joliffe. The return of the two ladies put an end to this confidential talk, and amid thanks given and received, the Paragreens left the Commissary's office, and immediately afterwards, the Exhibition.

"Upon my word," said Mrs. Paragreen, with a very heated face, "these French seamstresses are queer creatures. I never saw such an odd way as they have of mending dresses — if they had been told to search us, they could not have been — more preposterous."

"Preposterous! how, my dear?" asked Paragreen.

"Never you mind — how. No one, who hasn't gone through it as Ida and I have done, could have an idea of how it was. Hadn't they the face, the saucy gipsies, to pretend that the poor girl's dress was torn also, looking for the tears that didn't exist, here, and there, and everywhere? I declare to goodness, that it was a downright search of our persons."

And so it was. Thanks to their jupes à la Malakoff, Mrs. Paragreen and Ida had been thoroughly searched from head to foot. But this demands a word or two of explanation. It must be known, that during the last few days a good number of the articles in the Exhibition had been stolen, among others a meerschaum pipe purchased by His Imperial Majesty; and in spite of the strictest vigilance, not one of the authors of these thefts could be discovered. The

French police, however, had their reasons for suspecting that some at least of these clever substractions were imputable to talented British individuals of the stronger sex, aided and abetted by female accomplices, who took advantage of the allowable fashionable amplitude of their garments, to conceal and carry off the plunder. Pity it is, that there can be no great good without some little admixture of evil! The broad stream of British NOBILITY and GENTRY, flowing towards the Paris Exhibition, had carried along with it, as even the noblest and clearest of rivers are apt to do, some impure particles — that is, to speak plainly, some of the sharpest members of the respectable brotherhood of the SWELL MOB.

Pretty certain of this fact, then, the French Police asked the English Police to send over some of their detectives, two of whom constantly mounted guard in the Rotunda. The fabulous circumference of Mrs. and Miss Paragreen, added to their obstinacy in remaining for hours in the Rotunda, had already aroused the attention of the English police officers when the information reached them, that a costly Sèvres cup had just been stolen out of that very place. The detectives at once singled out the two ladies on whom they had been keeping an eye, as in some way or other connected with the robbery. Availing themselves of the repeated rush of people up to the platform, they got near mother and daughter, and tried to ascertain if there were anything suspicious under the aristocratic folds of their garments. Common methods failing them, they had hit upon the uncommon one of rending asunder "the good eight guinea gown," and upon the farce that followed, — which, while establishing the innocence of mother and daughter, gave them such droll ideas of French seamstresses, and of their way of mending dresses.

CHAPTER XII.

At Corazza's.

The clock of the Palais Royal was striking half-past five, as our phalanx made their entrance into the Café Corazza, with the step and mien of people perfectly determined to dine — a determination, however, not so easily to be carried into effect, unless they took a table by storm, for there was not one among all the many in the room unoccupied.

While Mr. Paragreen, rather disconcerted by the general attention called forth by his own green hat, and the ladies' Brown Broad Brims, was pointing his eye-glass east, west, north, and south, a lady in a gorgeous silk dress, with flounce upon flounce, came up to him, and said something in a very civil voice. Mr. Paragreen rather wondered what such a magnificent person could want with him, but faithful to his principles of gallantry to the fair sex, made her his best bow; the lady, who was the Dame du comptoir, then repeated, "Par ici, Monsieur," and with a gesture that translated her words, showed them a small door. Mr. Paragreen manœuvred his party to the indicated spot, and found there a waiter, who led the way up stairs to an entre-sol, and through another large room full of persons, all busy dining, ushered them into what might be termed a light closet, where as yet there was no one. The ceiling was very low, and it was close and hot, but richly and tastefully fitted up.

"All right," exclaimed Mr. Paragreen, rubbing his hands, and taking possession of the largest of the tables, already laid for dinner — "if we miss the sight and bustle of what is going on down stairs, here we have privacy, and no one to look at us." Mr. Paragreen took off his green hat, and put it under his chair. "Now, let us enjoy ourselves."

The waiter handed Mr. Paragreen the printed "Carte du Restaurant," a pencil and a slip of paper.

"Pourquoi?" asked the Englishman, staring at the three articles.

"Pour écrire le menu de votre dîner, Monsieur," answered the waiter, and disappeared.

"Let us see," said Mr. Paragreen. "Bless my soul! what a confusion — Potages à la Julienne — au riz — au vermicelle — aux macaroni" — ("Faugh!" cried Mrs. Paragreen, in disgust.) "Bisque aux écrevisses — what do you say to that? — good — we'll put it down then. Shall we have 'anguilles à la tartare?'"

"What is that?" said Mrs. Paragreen.

"Why, I don't know — it looks well in print."

"Suppose it's only another name for frogs."

"Oh, frogs, my dear, have only one name, greenowls, you know — however, we won't have the tartares. — Ah! here's something capital — pâté de foie gras."

"And potatoes, pa," put in Tobo, a great amateur of that tubercle.

"Pâté de foie gras," wrote Mr. Paragreen, "aux pommes de terre."

And thus, putting one dish after the other to the vote, for no other reason than its looking well in print, and having it accepted or refused, merely as it sounded pleasantly, or unpleasantly, Mr. Paragreen succeeded in concocting a menu, enough to have raised Mr. Vatel from his grave, and caused him to commit suicide over again.

The waiter cast the glance of a critic over the paper, and uttered these words full of wondering reproach — "Vous ne voulez donc pas de rôti, Monsieur?"

"Oh oui, rôti, to be sure," said Mr. Paragreen, embarrassed.

"Faut-il vous commander des brochettes d'ortolans?"

"Oui, trés bun, brochettes d'ortolongs — et," — proceeded Mr. Paragreen, "cette chose, you know, vous savez, I mean — cette chose qui est si grosse et" — and to illustrate his meaning, he puffed out his cheeks, and began blowing away as if he were a pair of bellows.

"Omelette soufflée," said this Œdipus, to whom such inquiries had been propounded hundreds of times before, "omelette soufflée."

"That is it," applauded Mr. Paragreen, "homelette softy — I wonder what brotchets are," said Mr. Paragreen, as the waiter turned to go away.

"Et quel vin prenez vous?" asked the man, returning.

"Champagne frappé," said Mr. Paragreen majestically, firing off his great gun, and watching the countenance of the waiter to see the effect of his long-prepared shot. The waiter, however, had strong nerves, for not a muscle moved.

While the whole hungry family were staying their appetites with an occasional mouthful of bread, in walked a gentleman above the medium height and breadth, and seated himself at one of the small tables. He was in black, with a thin white muslin cravat, well-dressed and well-looking, for he had regular features, but in spite of dress and features, there was about him something repulsive; perhaps the fault lay in his massy black beard.

"Where have I seen that face before, I wonder," whispered Mr. Paragreen, "I am sure I have seen it, and not long ago either." However, it was not worth thinking about, for, the gentleman having raised his hat on entering the room, father, mother, and children at once set him down as a shopkeeper.

The new comer drew a letter from his pocket, read it over, with knitted brows, now laying it down, now taking it up again, and giving every possible sign of being annoyed by its contents.

"I remember now where I saw him," whispered Mr. Paragreen anew, "it was at the Exhibition, near the china shop of that brute of a fellow." The appearance of the potage broke the thread of Mr. Paragreen's recollections, and the six fell to eating with a sort of wild curiosity.

"Monstrous good, isn't it?" interrogated Mr. Paragreen.

"Delicious!" returned Mrs. Paragreen, holding out her plate for more.

"Joliffe is a knowing one," chuckled our good-natured little friend, "hasn't he a nose for what's good!"

As the words were passing Mr. Paragreen's lips, a dashing young man with carroty whiskers, and hair parted and laid flat and frizzled in the very height of fashion, his glass stuck in his eye, sauntered in, and going up to him of the black beard, ex-

claimed, with an unmistakable English twang,
"Comment ça va, Marquis?"

"Not well at all, my lord," answered the Marquis
in English, but with a detestable French accent, and
shaking the hand proffered; "I am sent for to London,
and must start at once -- it is very contrariant --
see for yourself," giving the letter.

His Lordship read the missive, and said, "Après
tout, ce n'est que deux jours — juste le temps de
donner une signature, et revenir."

"The worse for that," remarked the Marquis —
"and to have to stay at the Duke's twenty-four hours
— that's an age for me, I tell you — you know that
I don't like his Grace."

"N'importe. Les affaires sont les affaires. Une
signature, qui vous donne un château, et un parc
superbe — Dieu me damne! vous êtes difficile."

The Paragreens followed this conversation with
interest, not because the discourse was of dukes,
castles, and parks, but because two noblemen were
the interlocutors. To be sure, a mere French Marquis could not be of much importance to people who
had a Prince, so to say, for their intimate friend;

but to breathe the same atmosphere, to feed perhaps on the same potages and brochettes as a Lord — a real English Lord, that was a treat they could not hope for every day. As to his being a real Lord, that was self-evident, they could have sworn to the fact. Only remark the ease with which he dangles his cane, and the noble freedom with which he scans, through his glass, the features of the grown-up ladies present — such ease and freedom could belong to none but a Lord.

His Lordship having stared at the feminine part of our family to his heart's content, now condescends to cast his aristocratic eyes over their masculine accompaniment — his glance lingers a moment on Mr. Paragreen, when, lo! as if electrified, his Lordship starts forwards, crying with outstretched hands, "Sir Andrew! — by Jove! — delighted — how long have you been in Paris?"

The chief of the Paragreens, half proud, half abashed, regrets he has not the honour — there is a mistake — and bowing low, he begs to make himself known to his Lordship as Mr. Paragreen, of Eden Villa, Peckham.

"Is it possible? I beg a thousand pardons — Really, were it not for the voice, I should imagine it was Sir Andrew giving me the cut direct — Sir Andrew Narquotick, M. P. for Dumbshire — very likely you know him — I never saw such a likeness. 'Pon my word, it is ridiculous, one drop of water is not more like another drop of water, than you are to the worthy baronet."

"Uncommonly odd," quoth Mr. Paragreen, rather agreeably tickled at being the living portrait of a Baronet and M. P.

The young nobleman hopes he may be forgiven his intrusion, (energetic No — noes! and assurances that it is quite the reverse, "an honour,") supposes Mr. Paragreen and his charming family (bows and smiles from the ladies) have come over to see the Exhibition, (emphatic signs of assent,) and my lord renewing his apologies, gracefully inclines his head, and falls back to his own table.

The two noble friends being served by this time, began eating like common mortals, and the Paragreens following the good example, there was no thing to be heard for a little while, but the clatter and jingle of knives and forks, and the smacking of lips, diversified by the merry popping of corks. Presently the waiter brought in a reinforcement of champagne for the small table, and on a tray eight capacious wine-glasses. His Lordship desired the glasses to be filled, then turning to Mr. Paragreen, he said, "Will you do us the honour to join us in drinking Her Most Gracious Majesty's health?" A toast to Her Most Gracious Majesty can never be refused, so the six Paragreens rose, as did the Marquis, and my Lord, and the eight drank Queen Victoria's health with the greatest enthusiasm.

After this there came a second calm, and a good deal of whispering occurred between Mr. Paragreen and the waiter, the result of which was, that this official brought in a fresh supply of champagne, and a second tray, with a second load of glasses for the large table. Mr. Paragreen had a pride of his own, and was not going to be behindhand with any one — no — not with the best lord living. Facing round to the small table, he said, laying a certain stress on each word — "May I now beg of you, gentlemen, to drink the toast I am about to propose? To our powerful Ally, the Emperor of the French, and to the August Lady who adorns the French throne by her beauty and virtues."

"With the most heartfelt pleasure," replied the personages addressed, and this toast was drunk quite as enthusiastically as the first.

The champagne had the effect of rendering the two parties more familiar with one another, and the fire of talk from one table to the other almost incessant. The Paragreens thus learned, that the Marquis was the son-in-law of his Grace the Duke of Shaughtbred, and that the object of his journey to England was to take possession, on his wife's behalf, of some property lately bequeathed to her by an uncle. Meanwhile both dinners were drawing towards their close.

"It is growing late, my dear," said the Marquis, rising, "and I must see about the money — with your leave," and away he went.

"My friend," condescendingly explained the young lord, though the Marquis had always spoken in English, "is gone to look for Bank of England notes in exchange for his French billets de banque

—very disagreeable, the money being different in the two countries."

To this Mr. Paragreen perfectly agreed. My lord sat on crunching biscuits and cracking nuts, but said nothing further. Ten minutes had scarcely elapsed when the Marquis returned, a magnificent red and gold pocket-book in his hand, and looking very much chafed. "The devil take these changers of money, and their saint also," he exclaimed, throwing himself into a chair, "not one of their sacré shops open." The rest of the explanation was only for his lordship's ear.

"What strange coincidences there are in life!" said this last, in a thoughtful way, to Mr. Paragreen. "It seems that to-day is the fête of the Patron Saint of money-changers, and all their places of business being closed, my friend cannot get the bank-notes he requires."

"He will find plenty of them at Bolone," remarked Mr. Paragreen.

"But, my dear friend, I arrive at Boulogne at three in the morning, and sail immediately," said the Marquis. "How am I to do?"

Mr. Paragreen gave a hem! "I think I have some of the goods you are in search of here," observed he, with the affected carelessness of a purse-proud man; and producing his well-lined, sober-coloured pocket-book, — "How much do you want?"

"Forty pounds at least," answered the Marquis, "as I have no French bills under thousand francs."

"Here's your money," said Mr. Paragreen, handing over two twenty-pound notes.

"Thank you very much," returned the Marquis, putting them into his pocket-book, and giving Mr. Paragreen a French note for a thousand francs. "Thank you very much, sir; you render me a great service. I must see more of you. Will you do me the pleasure of eating a soup with me — quite sans façon? I want to introduce you to Lady Clara, my wife. Ah! here's a bill for five hundred francs. I thought I had none under a thousand. Perhaps you will not mind giving me twenty pounds more for this? You spare me the trouble of going to a money-changer in London."

"Very good," replied Mr. Paragreen, giving a

couple of ten-pound notes, and receiving the one for five hundred francs.

"Thank you. Now name your day, if you please. Let me see — to-day is Friday — Saturday, Sunday, and Monday — yes, let it be Monday. I shall be back on Monday morning — half-past six o'clock exact. Do you promise?"

Mr. Paragreen promised.

"Thank you. I then rely on you, and all your family. But I must be gone. Good bye — half-past six — here is my card."

And after a cordial shake of the hand with both Mr. and Mrs. Paragreen, Marquis and Lord went off in high glee apparently, for their hearty peals of laughter, as they went down stairs, were distinctly audible to those they had just quitted.

"Merry dogs," said Mr. Paragreen, sympathizingly. "Now, then, let me see," and he read aloud from the bit of pasteboard he held, "'Marquis de la Motte d'Or, Rue Las Cases, No. 43.' So, so, we are going to dine with a real Marquis, and most probably his lordship will be of the party. How easily high connexions are formed in this country — in such an off-hand way too!"

"Yes, dear boy," replied Mrs. Paragreen, "if we were going to stay a month — only a month in Paris — there's no saying where we might not get our foot in."

"Hum! We must find out this Rue Las Cases, and leave a card for the Marquis, that he may know that we are not nobodies, but have a place of our own, though we ain't lords or dukes. Think of our taking him for a shopkeeper!"

"Well, I can't say he looks much as if he belonged to the aristocracy; but he's a foreigner, you know. His Lordship quite threw him into the shade — such a difference to my mind. His Lordship has much more ease of manner, and speaks better."

"Yes, Dora, you are right; he looks the nobleman from head to foot, and no mistake. I wonder what is his title?"

Thanks to the champagne, and the still more intoxicating draught administered to their vanity, the senior Paragreens saw everything through rose-coloured glasses — even the bill, though it was heavier than they expected. The galleries of the Palais Royal were all in a blaze when they left Corazza's, and the gardens crowded. The glittering of the shops, the sparkling of the fountains, the animation of the company, made up a scene of splendour, most gladdening to the eyes of our dear friends.

They enjoyed it to the utmost, then, with slow and lingering steps, took their way home by the Rue Vivienne, went into Galignani's for five minutes, to allow of Mrs. Paragreen's getting some of the last numbers of Galignani's Messenger, for purposes best known to herself, and Mr. Paragreen one of the last novels to read at home, and along the Boulevard des Italiens, and that of the Capucines, came to their hotel, old and young agreeing that it had been all perfectly delightful, and that there was no café in the world that could be compared with the Café CORAZZA.

CHAPTER XIII.

Jacques Bonhomme.

SUPPOSE we take the children to this Boa de Bolone Tobo tells us such wonders about?" This motion was made at breakfast on the Saturday morning by Mrs. Paragreen, who, since her misadventure in the Rotunda, had lost some of her partiality for the "*Diagmans de Couronne.*"

"And on our way to the Boa we might leave a card at No. 43 in the Rue Las Cases," suggested Mr. Paragreen.

"If the Roo is on our way to the Boa," observed Mrs. Paragreen; a prudent reservation — for, on consulting the Paris map, it proved that the Rue Las Cases was quite in an opposite direction.

"Never mind," said sagacious Mr. Paragreen, "all roads lead to Rome, you know. We'll take a fly by the hour, drive first to the Rue, and when we get to the Boa we can send it away."

"Isn't it nice, just?" cried Emma and Arabella, making a rush for their hats.

But Mr. Paragreen, with all his sagacity, had more than one thing to learn on this day, for, when they came to where he had hired his cab to go to the Jardin d'Hiver, he was made to understand that there existed a police regulation which only allowed of four persons at a time in a double-seated fly. As the case stood, therefore, the choice lay between going on foot or having two coaches.

"In for a penny, in for a pound," said Mr. Paragreen briskly, as his eye fell on the two little girls, whose faces expressed the extreme of agitated suspense. "What's the use of higgling about spending a few shillings for our own comfort, when" — Mr. Paragreen either left the phrase unfinished, or his words were drowned by the noise of the two coaches setting off.

Few persons ever passed No. 43 in the Rue Las Cases, when the porte-cochère was open, a very rare occurrence indeed, without being struck by the elegance and snugness of the small hotel situated at the further end of the front court. It is a modern structure, intended evidently only to accommodate a small family, for the main part of the building consists but of two stories, and the wings simply of a ground floor. The centre is surmounted by a cupola, which gives the mansion something the air of a temple — the temple of comfort, perhaps. The flowers and shrubs in bloom, let the season of the year be what it might, which border the double flight of steps leading up to the front door — the door itself of plate glass, shining as a mirror — the snow-white muslin curtains, with their delicate rose-coloured draperies, shading the windows; in short, all that the passer-by can take in at a glance, has about it a witching charm, that more than once tempted the chronicler of the Paragreens to break the Tenth Commandment, by saying to himself, I wish that house was mine!

There being nobody visible in the porter's lodge to receive his cards, though a sound of forks and plates close by showed that there were inmates at hand, Mr. Paragreen manfully called out "Portier!"

"Qu'est-ce que c'est?" grunted a coarse voice in resentful tones, and following on the sound appeared from an inner room a swarthy ill-favoured colossus, with eye-brows as thick and projecting as the moustache of the best beard-furnished French grenadier. "Il n'y a pas de portier ici." This was said with sharp brevity, the eye-brows meeting and lowering most ominously.

"Pas de portier?" echoed Mr. Paragreen interrogatively, exhibiting his visiting cards.

"Non, Monsieur," replied the man sternly, "il y a un Con-cierrrrr-ge," (had he said instead "Emperor," the speaker could not have accentuated the word more,) "et c'est moi."

Mr. Paragreen did not see the distinction, but he had no inclination to dispute the point, so he handed his cards, saying, "Pour le Marquis de la Motte d'Or."

"Sorti" was the brief rejoinder.

"Oui, parti pour Londres, je sais," exclaimed Mr. Paragreen, with a capable air.

"Je dis *sorti* et non *parti*," growled the Cerberus most distinctly, and, shrugging his shoulders with a look of disgust at the visitor, he slowly withdrew into his inner den.

"A pleasant little place, I must own," said Mrs. Paragreen, casting a parting glance through the porte-cochère.

"Yes, very — but such a porter I never did see; just like a wild beast — does not even understand French."

"As to that, Sylvester, my dear," returned the lady, jokingly, "it is no great wonder if he does not understand yours."

"Ha! well — laugh away at my French as you please," said the husband in the same jocular tone, "but for all that I have got it here," tapping his forehead.

"Yes, in the same place, I suppose, with the plan of Paris."

"Very good," cried the husband, with a hearty laugh, "well done, Dora — capital hit, upon my word."

A proud and happy husband and father did Mr. Paragreen feel himself as he handed his fair partner and his girls out of their respective carriages at the Porte Maillot. We do not ourselves much care to read, and much less still to write, descriptions of parks or palaces, so we shall leave the Bois de Boulogne, its lake, cascades, châlets, &c., undescribed, limiting ourselves to the statement that the Paragreens had a two hours' delicious stroll through its shades and winding paths, together with a little excursion on the water, Tobo pulling the stroke-oar in gallant style. When it was time to think of leaving, Mr. Paragreen proposed that, for the sake of variety, they should go back by the Avenue de l'Impératrice and the Arc de l'Etoile, instead of returning to Paris by the way they had come. It was just at that period, as everybody knows, that the avenue named after the Empress was thrown open to the public, unfinished as it was, and thronged with masons, bricklayers, paviers, and labourers employed in levelling the ground.

Through this new thoroughfare, then, the Paragreens, with their hop and stride, proceeded, not as usual, three abreast, but Mr. Paragreen with Tobo and the two little girls, and Mrs. Paragreen arm-in-arm with Ida, distinctly bent on a tête-à-tête. Mrs. Paragreen had been neither blind nor indifferent to the half-suppressed sighs heaving the bosom of her pretty daughter, as she reviewed a scene but so lately visited with a too charming cicerone; and seeing and observing, all the mother awoke in Mrs. Paragreen, impelling her to bestow comfort where it was needed. And thus it came to pass that she abruptly burst forth with, "What the *jeuse* can be the meaning of that good-for-nothing fellow not making his appearance?"

"What good-for-nothing fellow, mamma?"

"You know very well, Ida, whom I mean, the dandy with the brougham and fine horse. I begin to suspect you must have thrown him back."

"O no, mamma! at least I don't think I did; I am sure I never intended it — mamma!"

This last exclamation was one of mingled surprise and delight; for, — as Mrs. Paragreen afterwards observed, "speak of you know who, you know, and he is sure to appear," — there, sweeping by them like a meteor, was the identical brougham, and its grand chestnut horse, the owner's fair head and face, tuft on the chin and all, bowing with hurried grace, and, in a smile of recognition, letting fall the fragrant weed from his rosy lips.

"I see I must take this matter into my own hands," said Mrs. Paragreen, as she watched the colour flutter and then fade from Ida's cheek. "I must and will, for I'll allow no one, not the Pope himself, to trifle with my daughter's feelings — a little hop-o'-my-thumb. — Gracious me, I declare it is raining."

"So it is, and I have got my blue silk on!" cried Ida, in consternation. "It was so fine only a minute ago."

The few large drops of rain which had attracted Mrs. Paragreen's attention soon increased to a regular heavy summer shower, against which the ladies' parasols were of little or no avail. "This way — follow me!" shouted Mr. Paragreen, galloping off with the children and Tobo towards a small building about a hundred paces distant by the side of the road, and the only shelter visible in all the cleared-away space; — "make haste." They did run as fast as they could, and were soon under cover of the widely projecting eaves of a small wooden house, or rather shed, for it was, in fact, nothing but a mere temporary tavern or public-house, erected for the accommodation of the men at work in the Avenue, groups of whom were converging from all points thither at this very moment of time. The violence of the rain augmenting, and the roof proving but a poor shelter, Mr. Paragreen saw no reason why he and his should not do as they had seen many others do.

Accordingly, they went inside into a large naked room, the only furniture of which was a set of rough deal tables, with wooden benches round them, and most of the seats and tables already occupied by working men, many of them drinking. Mr. Paragreen espying an empty table at the furthest end of the room from the door, led the way to it, the ladies taking possession of the bench, while the gentlemen seated themselves on the table. It is next to useless to add that the father and son no more thought of raising their hats on entering than of bowing to the lamp-posts in the street.

Now, Jacques Bonhomme is the politest of men. He never goes into a café, a restaurant, a shop, an omnibus, a railway carriage, or a railway waiting-room, any place, in short, where human beings are

congregated, without at least touching his head-gear.
But exactly because the best bred of men, the
Frenchman is also the most sensitive to any neglect
of the forms of civility, especially so when he belongs
to those labouring classes, which nowhere feel their
importance, and the respect they are entitled to,
more than in France, and particularly in Paris. On
the score of politeness, the Parisian artisan is most
ticklish and exacting. It is not to be wondered at,
then, if the advent of Mr. Paragreen handling his
eye-glass, with green hat immovable, and his head
waving with a patronizing air from side to side,
awakened feelings of irritation among the present
company, who took this sort of behaviour for an
intentional bravado. Mr. Paragreen, on his part,
was quite at a loss to account for the hostility of
the glances he encountered, and still less could he
assign a cause for the threatening attitude assumed
by a young mason, who, backed by five or six other
men, and soon joined by most of the rest, advanced
on a sudden towards him, and crossing his arms over
his breast, exclaimed, "Ah! ça, dites donc, sacre
muffle!"

"Plait-il?" said Mr. Paragreen, looking benignantly at the speaker.

"Aviez-vous peur de vous désarticuler le bras en saluant des Chrétiens?" pursued the other.

This was Sanscrit to our little man, who, however, perceived the urgency of saying something conciliatory, and bethought himself of that which had done him such good service on other occasions, so he replied, "Anglais — Alliés."

"Alliés tant que vous voudrez," answered the Frenchman, somewhat softened, "mais au moins il faudrait y mettre de la politesse. Voyons—allez-vous ôter ce champignon, oui ou non?"

Had he said "chapeau," ten to one but Mr. Paragreen would have been enlightened as to the true cause and front of his offending, but of the word "champignon" (the famous green hat was not unlike one) Mr. Paragreen could make neither head nor tail.

No satisfaction, or even answer, being vouchsafed, the mason made a dash at the green hat, but without success, its owner having jumped back in time. Mr. Paragreen, who was miles away from any conception of the reason of the Frenchman's conduct, but naturally enough saw in it a most unjustifiable assault, fired up in his turn. Every drop of blood in his veins tingled, bringing back a gleam, a feeling, a whiff of old times — of school, bundles of books, boxing, and black eyes. "At them, Tobo, my boy, Old England for ever, hurra!" shouted the little man, doubling his fists and squaring; "come on, my fine fellow." Tobo, delighted at the spree, stripped off his jacket in a twinkling, and threw himself into a scientific attitude, while Mrs. Paragreen, giving the table a violent push, with the spring of a tigress forced herself between her husband and son, the most dangerous-looking perhaps of the three. With flashing eyes, doubled fists, chests out, and backs in, they were really superb to look at. Ida, and her sisters from behind, thrust their parasols forward lancelike between the others, and never, since its formation, had the Macedonian phalanx presented so imposing a front.

This undaunted bearing, as if by magic, changed the feelings of the assailants. Bravery is a talisman of infallible effect with the brave. The Frenchman who is compelled to say of his antagonist, "il a du cœur," is already more than half disposed to shake hands with him. Things did not go so far as this, however, in the present case, but the leader of the attack fell back a pace or two, and looked irresolute. This gave time for a few cooler heads to interfere. The young mason was surrounded, reasoned with, and gently forced away, as well as the more excited of his followers. By degrees, something like calm was restored, and the family were left standing with a clear space before them. Into this species of arena stepped a middle-aged workman, evidently one having authority over his fellows, who made a short, and, judging by the approving nods and murmurs it elicited from his hearers, a most instructive and impressive address to Mr. Paragreen. As far as we have been able to ascertain, this speech was a free paraphrase of Burns's famous line, "A man's a man for a' that." This done, the successful orator made a sweeping salutation with his cap, and went out to his work, as did the rest, each man, half in sport, half in irony, using the same gesture, and the Paragreens were left alone in mute wonder. Mrs. Paragreen smoothed down her ruffled feathers, Tobo put on his jacket, and the whole party, glad to find that the rain had ceased, made their retreat in good order.

"What a set of savages!" exclaimed Mrs. Paragreen, when she found herself safe in the open air.

"Dash me! if I can make it out," returned her husband, his blood still on the boil; "it was a mercy that they had sense enough to discover that they had difficult customers to deal with."

"Yes, you behaved like a man, I must say that for you, Sylvester," said Mrs. Paragreen, "and so did Tobo."

"You were the best man of us all, I believe, Dora dear; upon my word, I do not know who would have dared to face you. I am the father of a family, and like peace and order, but when the devil is roused within me" — a flourish of the hand rounded the sentence.

"I do wonder what could be their motive for attacking us in that way?"

"Who can tell? probably to rob us."

"Oh no! Papa," cried Ida and Tobo simultaneously, "they had not the look of thieves — they were very angry — we must have given them some offence."

"But how could we?" said Mr. Paragreen; "I am sure we were as polite as possible to them — Ha! I'll tell you what it was — democratic spirit, which hates the sight of well-dressed people; you saw that they took a dislike to us from the first."

"Well, perhaps you are right," observed Mrs. Paragreen doubtingly, "but I would give something to know what that grey-haired man meant by all the gibberish he said to us — he spoke from his heart, I could make that out. It's rather a pity, Sylvester, you lost your French on the Bolone Railway."

Our friends had a right to some compensation after this disagreeable mishap, and a very sweet one awaited them at dinner that day; for scarcely had they made their bows and courtesies to His Highness, when the Prince, in a clear, high-pitched voice, meant to be heard by every one at the table, said, "Mr. Pappagreen — Madam — I am delighted to see you and your charming family looking so well."

These words put an instantaneous stop to some significant smiles and whispers, with which the Paragreens' appearance had been saluted. Somehow or other, a vague rumour had got afloat among the company, that Mr. and Mrs. Paragreen, after pretending they were going to the fête at Versailles, had not been there at all, the Honourable A. Smallwhey protesting he had not seen them, which was very true, the Honourable not having been there himself.

The little levee held by the Prince after dinner, afforded another triumph to our family. His Highness conversed with them for full five minutes, and was heard to exhort them to prolong their stay in Paris for another week, as Paris would be very gay. His Highness made his wish to distinguish them conspicuous. What could be his motive? Was it connected or not with the request for a private interview on business, soon after received by Mr. Paragreen from the Prince's secretary?

Mr. Paragreen, not without a shudder at the recollection of the last "confidential communication," answered nevertheless courteously, that he was at the Secretary's service at all times, but that if the business was not of a very urgent nature, — which the Secretary allowed it was not — he, Mr. Paragreen, would prefer spending the next day, Sunday, quietly with his family, and postponing all affairs till Monday morning at nine o'clock; an arrangement agreed upon.

CHAPTER XIV.

Dinner in the Rue las Cases.

On Monday morning, at the appointed hour, there came a gentle tap at the door of what served for Tobo's bed-chamber by night, and the family sitting-room by day. Mr. Paragreen, on hearing this signal, threw down the book he had been reading, and went to meet Mr. Secretary half-way.

"Good morning, Mr. Pap — Paragreen, I am sorry to intrude on you so early, but I shall not detain you long, for of course you will not allow your Gracious Sovereign to leave the French capital without having another peep of her."

"Certainly not," affirmed Mr. Paragreen.

"Well, then, without any preamble, I must at once state openly and candidly that I am come to you for advice and guidance. I come to you because I am sure you are a man of discretion, experience, and connections — yes, sir, of powerful connections, and one, I trust, I am not mistaken in considering His Highness's friend."

"His Highness's great admirer and sincere well-wisher at least," returned Mr. Paragreen.

"Thank you; I have not the least doubt of it. It is strange, isn't it, the sudden likings one takes to people. Now, His Highness took a fancy to you all from the very first. I think you are aware of the regard he has for you. Only last night he was saying to me, 'I must get Mr. and Mrs. Paragreen introduced at the Tuileries; I must, even if I am obliged to ask it as a personal favour of His Majesty.'"

"His Highness, indeed, has always been kinder to us than we had any right to expect," observed Mr. Paragreen.

"That is your opinion. Allow me to differ from you. But I must not trespass on your time and patience. The affair — you understand that this is strictly confidential," (these words made Mr. Paragreen flush all over,) "indeed, His Highness, up to this moment, is absolutely ignorant of what I am going to confide to you."

"Very good, sir; you may depend on me."

"I know I can, and that is why I am here. Well, sir, if my memory does not fail me, His Highness did once mention to you a stupendous enterprise in contemplation, the profits of which can hardly be estimated, and in which he was urged and pressed to invest a certain sum."

"Scarcely touched on the subject," was the laconic reply.

"But he did touch on it, so I feel at liberty to speak to you about it. This undertaking is one by which it is intended to substitute for the bread now in common use another kind, purer, easier of digestion, more nourishing, and at a third of the present cost."

"Indeed! is it possible?" exclaimed Mr. Paragreen.

"Not only possible, my good sir, but already realized. Experiments have been made on a very large scale and they have answered extraordinarily well. I daresay you have heard of the dwarf palm, which infests the soil of Algeria to such an extent as to prevent colonization. Now, listen. We take that injurious shrub, sir, we pound it, reduce it to powder, mix with that powder a small proportion of ground rice, and our bread is made. The beauty of the thing is, that while on the one hand we dispense to the poor an article of primary necessity at a cheap rate, on the other we render whole tracts of hitherto waste lands available to agriculture. So both ways we confer an incalculable benefit on mankind. I leave it to you to judge now of whether the profits can be anything but immense."

"I see, I see! — And" (the question was put with some anxiety by Mr. Puragreen,) "is this dwarf palm tree so very abundant in Algeria?"

"Beyond all conception, sir; we have material enough there to furnish the whole world with bread for centuries to come."

"Bless my heart!" ejaculated the little man, now in real alarm, "what will come of our corn-growers!"

"Why," replied the secretary, shrugging his shoulders, "we shall be very sorry for them, but they must just grow something else, you know — we cannot sacrifice the good of the many for that of the few."

"But it will be the ruin of English agriculturists, Sir, the utter ruin."

"Not," said the secretary with a calm smile, "if English agriculturists take shares in time in the enterprise — it's only changing their capital from one security to another. But now to come to the point. I have it greatly at heart that His Highness should become a shareholder, and invest not less than five thousand pounds in the speculation, morally certain as I am, that in the course of two or three years it will give him a net income equal to the sum invested. I cannot doubt but that the Western Powers in the end will come out of this war victorious, and consequently, that His Highness's dominions will be eventually restored to him. Still, the struggle may last, God knows how long; and even in case of a peace, there are always delays — my fears may be exaggerated — I daresay they are — attachment is easily alarmed, you know — in short, I feel it my duty not to let slip so promising an opening without an attempt to profit by it. But how? when, alas! His Highness has not the first farthing of the five thousand pounds required!"

"You don't say so?" panted Mr. Paragreen, with deep feeling. "Don't you think that the weather is uncommonly hot this morning?"

"Not for the season, the thermometer only marks twenty centigrades in the shade. As I was saying, the question is how best to raise the money," pursued the secretary, "and here it is that your assistance may prove of so much use to the Prince." (Mr. Paragreen could have taken his oath that the mercury was up to boiling point.) "You must know that, when His Highness's Palace was sacked and plundered, and His Highness dragged to prison, (I will tell you the whole story one of these days, and all about his miraculous escape,) some of his faithful servants, myself among the number, succeeded in hiding, and carrying away a scanty few of the Crown Jewels. These remnants of ancient splendour His Highness would of course never part with — His Highness considers them as the property of the State — but he might be persuaded, I hope and believe, into pledging them for a sum of money."

"Nothing more easy," returned Mr. Paragreen, brisking up as if the weather had suddenly cooled, "nothing more easy; any large pawnbroker in London will manage the business for you at once."

"Not so easy, sir, as you think. The Jewels I am speaking of, are as well known in Europe as those belonging to the French or English Crown. His Highness is proud, not without reason, and for nothing in the world would he have it said that he had pawned his Crown Jewels. Just think how all the papers in the Russian interest would teem with calumnious hints, and of all the scandal such a disclosure would cause. Pawnbrokers, and all those sort of people, would never answer. Do you take me?"

"I am not sure that I do."

"We must be protected, sir, safe from all possible indiscretion, and to be so, we must not go to the trade. What we require is a person of undoubted respectability, one on whose secrecy we may rely — a friend, in short, who, in good faith, and without any sort of fuss, you know, *inter nos*, as I might say, takes the jewels with one hand, and counts out the £5000 with the other."

The bait was evidently too large, and would not do.

"You will hardly find a man out of trade to accommodate you," observed Mr. Paragreen, musingly. "Jewels are peculiarly liable to sudden falls in value — not easily turned into cash at any time, and five thousand pounds is a large sum — a large sum."

"One thousand, strictly speaking, might do for a first instalment," returned the secretary, who felt the expediency of reducing the bait to more swallowable proportions. "As to finding such a man as we require, with money to spare, and not in trade, I never dissembled to myself the difficulties of the undertaking, but I had hoped to overcome them by the help of a person in your position and with your connections."

"I don't say it can't be done," said Mr. Paragreen, still politely declining the bait, "particularly if you limit your demand to £1000; but the business will require time and consideration. I confess that, at this moment, I don't call to mind any one to whom I could recommend you to apply — but in my connection, which, as you say, is not a narrow one,

I may be able to meet with some one, in or out of trade, who will suit you. I will think over it, and let you know as soon as I can." (All the while, truth to say, Mr. Paragreen had his mental eye fixed on a little pawnbroker in Tottenham Court Road, with whom the ci-devant merchant had had little out-of-the-way analogous transactions, during his own business career.)

"I should not mind a trip to London," said the secretary, "if you thought it advisable. I should only be too happy to form one of your party."

"We should be delighted indeed."

"Perhaps you will give me leave to call again to-morrow morning — not that I mean to press you as to that matter, God forbid, but I should be so glad to see the charming little ones."

"You are always welcome, sir; we will say, if agreeable to you, ten o'clock, I mean after our breakfast."

Ten would answer exactly, and his secretaryship took his leave with a face of sunshine, but his inner man as black as ink. His hopes of the thousand pounds were so faint, that had he been offered a ten-pound note for his chance, he would have struck the bargain on the spot.

The family made a hurried breakfast, and reached the Boulevards early enough to have a full hour to wait, before they had the opportunity of wishing Her Majesty a good journey; that duty performed, they agreed upon going to see what the Exhibition of Fine Arts was like. But the Fine Arts did not answer at all. The Paragreens had scarcely gone through the room of English Painting, when Mrs. Paragreen declared it made her eyes ache, and was very tiring always to see the same thing over and over again, and that they had better go home. Accordingly they went home, and on their way ordered two carriages from the livery stables close by, to be at the Hotel at six o'clock precisely. The intervening hours were spent by mother and daughters in mysterious preparations for the dinner toilet, (the dinner at the Corazza's Marquis, you recollect.) Mr. Paragreen tried to finish the book bought at Galignani's, Tobo took the Galignani's Messengers purchased by his mother, and singled out for perusal all the murders, and poisonings, and other spicy matters, which was no sinecure.

It wanted but a minute of half-past six o'clock by Mr. Paragreen's watch, when the two coaches with himself and family, stopped at No. 43, Rue Las Cases, and coachman No. 1 alighting, gave a single knock at the porte-cochère.

"Gracious me!" exclaimed Mrs. Paragreen, "the man's a fool — only a single knock, what does he take *us* for?"

Without a word, Mr. Paragreen darted from the coach, grasped the knocker, and thundered forth such a rap as, since the world began, was never before heard out of Belgravia. The effect was instantaneous and tremendous. The porte-cochère expanded with a frightful clang, the latch continuing to jerk up and down, as if seized with frenzy. The glass door of the house crashed on its hinges, two footmen in lively alarm springing out on the steps. Shut windows opened, open windows opened wider, and from every aperture out came heads and cries both loud and shrill, of "What's the matter?" The loge vomited forth the shaggy-browed Cerberus, his wife, children, and stranger within his gates — all in a state of exasperation, and all of them together answering the calls from the glass door and windows; while by way of doing what he ought to do, a large dog in a kennel rushed forth, barking furiously, and tearing with all his might and main to get clear of his chain, and make mince meat of the intruders.

And amidst all this uproar and confusion, its unconscious cause, the Paragreen family, were seen moving up gravely, three abreast, towards the glass door.

The reception they met with from the footman was not over gracious. "The Marquis could not receive visitors at that hour," it was "l'heure de son dîner."

"Dinnère? très bong," cried Mr. Paragreen, most good-humouredly; "nous sommes pour dinnère also."

The little man's assured tone told on the servant, who, taking the card proffered by Mr. Paragreen, went into the house, and almost immediately returned to usher Monsieur and Madame Papagrand, as he announced them, into a large room, in which there were only two persons, a lady and gentleman — the very lady and gentleman — (now, don't say it is not true, because unlikely, — truth often is, you know) — who had travelled from Boulogne to Paris in the same carriage as the Paragreens, and to whom Mrs. Paragreen had so liberally granted a patent for vulgarity.

The first movement of both parties betrayed unfeigned surprise, mixed up on the part of our hero and heroine with *quantum suff* of mortification, on that of the other couple with a strong wish to laugh. There now, thought Mr. Paragreen, we go out once in a way to dinner, and just that once we must light on the only people we had rather not meet — and taking it for granted that these were other guests, polite enough they seemed after all, he said to the gentleman, who had advanced some steps towards him, "I hope the Marquis is well?"

"Quite well, I thank you," answered the gentleman, in tolerable English.

"He has had a good journey also, I trust," went on Mr. Paragreen, blandly.

"'Thank you," returned the other, as if he did not quite comprehend.

Having thus spoken, with a slight bow at the close of each sentence, while courtesies were being exchanged between Mrs. and Miss Paragreen and the stranger lady, Mr. Paragreen considered he had offered a sufficient sacrifice on the altar of civility; he therefore turned on his heels, and holding his glass to his eye, began to examine the pictures on the walls.

One of those furtive smiles and looks, full of fun nevertheless, which we have before noticed, now passed between the French lady and gentleman; then the latter, going up to Mr. Paragreen, said, "I beg your pardon for the question, but have you anything to communicate to the Marquis?"

"Nothing in particular, Sir," said Mr. Paragreen, resuming his examination.

"Surely your visit has an object?" insisted the Frenchman.

"Certainly, and a very pleasant one," answered the Englishman, rather superciliously; "that of dining with my Lord Marquis."

"Dining with the Marquis! Excuse me, Sir, do you know him personally?"

"Of course I do," said Mr. Paragreen, a little provoked at being thus cross-examined — "we received the invitation from his own lips."

"Then there must be some mistake, as I am the only Marquis of the name extant in France."

"*You?* — you the only Marquis de la Motte d'Or!" cried Mr. Paragreen in the greatest bewilderment. "And you haven't a brother, or son, or cousin, or some relation or other — a tall handsomish man of five-and-thirty, or forty, with a black beard, and who has the same name as you?"

"None," said the Marquis; "there is, I assure you, no other De la Motte d'Or but myself."

It was Mr. Paragreen's turn now to make excuses and beg pardon. He briefly related under what circumstances the invitation had been given, suppressing, however, the previous exchange of bank-notes, and then took out of his pocket, and showed the card he had received at Corazza's. It was, in fact, one of his own cards, said the real Marquis, and had certainly come from his own card-case, a rather valuable one which he had lost, or been robbed of not long ago; and he supposed that the person who had got it now, must be either a wag, who liked a joke, or more probably still, an adventurer, who was trading under the Marquis' name. Neither Mr. nor Mrs. Paragreen, however, would admit of this last hypothesis, and brought as unanswerable arguments against it the very distinguished appearance of the *soi-disant* Marquis, and his intimacy with an English Lord. On being asked the name of this lord, our friends were obliged to confess, to their great annoyance, that they did not exactly know the English nobleman's title, it not having, somehow or other, been once uttered by his companion; an omission which caused Monsieur de la Motte d'Or to stick more obstinately than ever to his opinion, that they had been duped by a chevalier d'Industrie.

The Marchioness perceiving that our friends were really shocked by such an idea, cleverly gave her husband a hint to let the subject drop, and said, though their coming was owing to a mistake, she hoped Mr. and Mrs. Paragreen would give her and her husband the benefit of that mistake, by cordially accepting a dinner very cordially offered. In this invitation the Marquis joined with a very good grace, and after a little skirmishing, mention of fear of intrusion, &c., on the part of our family, the polite proposal was agreed to, and Mrs. Paragreen and her daughters were shown into an adjoining boudoir, where they deposited their opera cloaks, and assured themselves that they were all right. They re-entered the salon in time to hear Monsieur le Général Comte d'Estong announced, and to identify in the Count the military-looking gentleman with the grey moustaches, and red rosette — the perpetrator of that salute which had so scandalized our Englishwoman. Introduced by the Marchioness to her impromptu guests as "My uncle," the new arrival not only repeated his former offence by kissing his niece's hand, but deliberately raised Mrs. Paragreen's also to his lips; nor did that lady now consider the compliment as a proof of such bad taste.

When they went to dinner, the Marquis handed in Mrs. Paragreen, (if he had only been an English

Marquis! thought Dora,) the Count took pretty Ida, and then the noble hostess, motioning to tall, sheepish Tobo to go on with his little sisters, followed herself, leaning on the arm of Mr. Paragreen, who sidled and flapped his wings, arms we mean, and hopped away more on tiptoe than ever.

The Marchioness, anxious to put her new acquaintances at their ease, carefully broached only those topics she supposed most calculated to interest them, such as the Queen's visit, the London Crystal Palace, the success of the English painters at the Exhibition of the Fine Arts, &c. The Count peppered the conversation, so to say, with his humorous sallies and facetious allusions to their meeting on the railway, but most of all with the drollest English ever spoken. "Anoder bumpère to our entière reconciliation, Mr. Paragrin, and let all rancune to de bouton of de glass. You were fachéd all red. Do not say non. If you had kept me into an egg, I was flambéd — you did me such eyes dat à la fin I must save myself."

Mr. Paragreen took everything in excellent part, and, with the exception of some occasional short fits of absence, made himself very agreeable. Thus, half between joke and earnest, the Paragreens came to understand how and why their three travelling companions had not to pass through the fiery ordeal of the waiting-room at Boulogne; the how and why being that Monsieur le Comte d'Estong held a high military command in the division in which Boulogne was situated, and that the railway managers had naturally wished to show a due regard to one of the first authorities in the Department, and to those with him.

The evening was enlivened by music. Uncle and niece began by playing one of Beethoven's sonatas for violin and piano, which threw Mr. and Mrs. Paragreen into raptures. The Marchioness also sung an air of Bellini's, and then Ida, being very much pressed, found enough courage to give them a Scotch ballad, with a simplicity that did her the greatest honour, and which received an unanimous encore. When at last Mr. and Mrs. Paragreen rose to take leave, the Marquis told them his britzka was at the door to take them home, — an unexpected attention, which called forth a perfect explosion of really sincere thanks, for of all the kindnesses they had received this last touched their hearts the most.

"Où allons nous?" asked the coachman.

"Palais Royal," answered Mr. Paragreen, without the least hesitation.

"Why, Sylvester, my dear," began Mrs. Paragreen.

"Palais Royal," reiterated Mr. Paragreen, whispering in his astonished mate's ear, "Not a word, I beg, we may be overheard — the whole of them seem to speak English."

Accordingly they drove to the Palais Royal in complete silence. Alighting here, Mr. Paragreen led them into the first gallery he saw, and began scanning the descriptive titles of the shops, now and then showing signs of impatience and disappointment, till he came to one closed, like all those which had been the peculiar object of his investigations, but through the chinks of the shutters of which light within was visible. Mr. Paragreen stopped and rapped, but, getting no answer, he gave the door a push and opened it. "Est-il bong?" said he, presenting to the startled inmate the two French bank-notes he had received at Corazza's.

"Trop tard," said the money-changer, "la caisse est fermée."

"Est-il bong, I say?" insisted Mr. Paragreen.

The man thus challenged took the notes, examined them narrowly, held them up between himself and the candle, and then articulated, "Excellents."

"Thank you, merci, monseer. All is safe!" shouted Mr. Paragreen, so loud that many of the passers by stood still an instant to look at our excited friend. "All's safe; and now I understand the whole business. Our own Marquis is the friend of the Marquis de la Motte d'Or, and had a card of his in his pocket-book, and gave it by mistake. It's as clear as day. Now, Dora, am I a practical man or not? No delay, you see — action — that's the thing."

No one disputed Mr. Paragreen being the most practical man of his day; and the taboo being raised, the family went home all taking at once over the marvellous events of the day.

CHAPTER XV.

Catastrophe Number One.

"STUFF and nonsense!" said Mr. Paragreen, as he threw down the book he had been reading.

"What's it about?" asked Mrs. Paragreen.

"The heroine, to begin with, an English young lady, falls in love at first sight with an Italian — so very likely!"

"Not so unlikely though," rejoined the lady. "Haven't I told you scores of times of Lizzy Paddiston, my friend at the Liddels' school, who went crazy about her singing-master, and married him into the bargain — and then wasn't there the only daughter of Admiral what's his name, who lived at Twickenham — didn't she fret herself into a consumption for the sake of an Italian she met at Nice? Lor, Mr. Paragreen, you don't know anything about girls and their ways."

"Well, well, you may be right as to the girl, I

don't pretend to understand your sex, but I know something about my own, and no one will persuade me that the father is not a mere caricature — an old English gentleman made out as obstinate, stiff-necked, and proud as a mule, turning up his nose at everything and everybody."

"As to that," replied Mrs. Paragreen, who was in a vein of contradiction, "I remember you saying yourself, that Sir Benjamin Mace the Morisons made such a fuss about, looked as if he had swallowed the poker — and I have not forgotten, if you have, that high and mighty M. P. we met in the lane near Oxford, who wouldn't tell us our way himself, but motioned to us to ask his groom."

"Exceptions, Dora; you may go the world over and find nothing to match a real fine English gentleman; after all, we are none of us so bad as we seem, that's my opinion. Then, bless your heart, there's such a deal of politics — all well in a newspaper, but out of place in a novel. First, I hate to be made miserable by way of amusement; then how can I tell the fact from the fiction? If Italian patriots are really hanged and sent to the galleys, and what not, come to me with a plain business-like statement, and no sentimental humbug about it — and like a freeborn Briton I will lend them a hand — I will, by jingo, — though I hardly know what kind of chaps these Italians are."

"Why, dear me!" exclaimed Mrs. Paragreen, "how can you say so, after making such a work about those Sardinian navy officers you met in London the other day? — to hear you, there wasn't anything like them in the world."

"And very gentlemanly they were, and quite above the common run; but our gallant allies, the Sardinians, my dear, are not Italians."

"They talk Italian at all events," said Mrs. Paragreen, whose notions were, perhaps, owing to Miss Liddels' boarding-school, less misty as to nationalities than her husband's. "Well, what next?"

"A parcel of absurdities — the heroine is all for love in a cottage, and says she doesn't care for rank and court — and she is rich you know, and noble, and brought up to all that sort of thing."

"That's all bosh!" pronounced Mrs. Paragreen with great decision.

"Bosh!" repeated Mr. Paragreen; "Dora, my dear, I do wish you wouldn't say *bosh*,— it's a vulgar word — you ought to know that, you who are so sharp in detecting vulgarity."

Mr. Paragreen had had this sentiment on the tip of his tongue ever since the discovery of the rank of their travelling companions, so unequivocally set down as "vulgar" by his spouse.

"How nice we have grown!" said Mrs. Paragreen tartly; "I remember somebody in the cork line saying *arter*, when he was paying his addresses —

"To somebody in the drysalter line," finished off Mr. Paragreen.

He was terrified at the sound of his own words, and gave himself up for lost.

Mrs. Paragreen looked at him with that dreadful smile of hers — looked at him for a second, as if she would make only one morsel of him, then said with appalling composure, — "Will you be so kind as to tell me the time by your watch, Mr. Paragreen?"

Mr. Paragreen hastened to answer the ominous query; it wanted exactly twenty minutes to eleven.

"Thank you. I think a little walk in the open air will do you good, Mr. Paragreen. Perhaps you will have the goodness to take Tobo and the children with you, and let me have the pleasure of seeing you here again at two o'clock precisely."

Mr. Paragreen summoned Tobo and the children, and decamped without another word.

As soon as they were gone, Mrs. Paragreen and Ida put on their broad brims, and went in a coach to the Rue de Rivoli. Over the windows of the first floor of the house at which they stopped, was a large sign-board, with this inscription in large golden letters,—

MR. SHUFFREY, MÉDECIN DENTISTE,
SURGEON DENTIST.

Mr. Shuffrey, the reader need scarcely be told, was the celebrated inventor of the far-famed "Galvano-Plasto-Mastodon-Self-Masticating Râteliers," which figured at the Paris Exhibition, and for which the Commissioners awarded the Great Gold Medal to the inventor. Now, a trifle being the matter with one of Ida's front teeth, her mother prudently wished to have it put to rights abroad rather than at home. Anxious to find out a fashionable and respectable dentist, without committing herself by questioning any of the ladies of the table-d'hôte, Mrs. Paragreen had bought that set of Galignani's Messenger on their way home from Corazza's, and in her diligent study of the same, had lighted on the following paragraph, headed —

"SERIOUS ACCIDENT at the Palace of Industry.— The rush of people to see the famous MR. SHUFFREY'S wonderful SELF-MASTICATORS was such yesterday, that several ladies met with serious injuries — happily, no loss of life to be deplored — and consequently the Police of the Palais de l'Industrie have thought it necessary to place a number of Sergens de Ville round the counter, so as to keep the circulation in that quarter free."

This paragraph had put an end to Mrs. Paragreen's irresolution, and she had managed, by means of epistolary correspondence, to make an appointment, unknown to her husband, with this great artist for eleven o'clock in the forenoon of this present Tuesday.

Our two ladies were shown into a gorgeously furnished drawing-room, by a footman in a gorgeous livery, who took their names, and soon after, on the ringing of a little bell, they were introduced by a small groom in top boots, into the *sancta sanctorum*. The *genius loci* was stooping down over a table examining something through a microscope, when they entered. The rustling of the silk dresses made the absorbed operator raise his head, and turn towards the door. No sooner did mother and daughter catch a sight of his face, than they stood still as if rooted to the ground, Ida with a faint cry, seeking her mother's hand. Mr. Shuffrey, on his side, evinced symptoms of the greatest agitation, reddened, showed the white of his eyes, and finally laid both his hands on his heart.

The first to recover some self-possession was Mrs. Paragreen, who began thus — "Sir, it is not my intention to investigate by what means you became aware of our having an appointment here, and have succeeded in penetrating into this place — nor shall I add to your confusion by questioning the delicacy and propriety of such a proceeding. I know what love is, and am disposed to be even over-lenient in love matters. — All I have to say is, that since you are here and I am not sorry you are, I shall take the opportunity of speaking a few serious words to you."

"I shall only be too happy, Madam," replied Mr. Shuffrey with emotion, "to hear anything you may desire to say. But will you not take a seat?"

"No seats, thank you. It shall be done in a moment. Only answer me this question, What are your intentions, sir?"

"My intentions, Madam!" stammered Mr. Shuffrey.

"No ambiguity, sir. — I mean, sir, what are your intentions with regard to this daughter of mine — Miss Paragreen, sir?"

"Oh, madam! the purest, the most honourable — the — could you ever doubt what they were? Here — I place at this lovely angel's feet my heart, my name, my fortune. Speak out, fair maiden. My bliss or misery hangs on your words. Decide my fate, whatever it be, and life or death, it shall be welcome from your lips." And to give force to this intimation, Mr. Shuffrey bent one knee before Ida, and hid his face in his hands.

"I wish you would get up," said Mrs. Paragreen, helping the young gentleman to his feet. "Your speech is rather a flowery one, but it is the speech of a gentleman. However, before we say any more about bliss and misery, you can understand that it is but natural in a parent to wish to know something more positive about yourself and your prospects in life."

"It is not for me to descant on my name," answered Mr. Shuffrey, with a little bow in compliment to it. "You know, Madam, that it is not an unhonoured one. As to my means, they allow me to cut a good figure in the world, as you see," looking proudly round the room. "My one-horse brougham will very soon be exchanged for a britzka and pair, my practice increases every day, and such is the success of my self-masticators"—

"Mercy on us!" cried Mrs. Paragreen, recoiling

in sudden horror, "you, then, are — that — abominable Mr. Shuffrey!"

"Abominable! Madam" —

"Yes, abominable! — a dentist! — worse than a veterinary surgeon. And you fancy that I am going to throw away my daughter on a low tooth-drawing apothecary like you?"

"Madam" —

"A Miss PARAGREEN, sir!—her mother a JOLIFFE, sir!" concluded Mrs. Paragreen, drawing herself up, and looking most majestic.

"Madam," said Mr. Shuffrey, in an agitated voice, "you can break my heart, but you cannot throw disgrace on a profession of which I am proud — yes — proud, and but for which" — with the look of a connoisseur at the angry lady's mouth — "and but for which you would be a downright scarecrow, madam."

"Come away, Ida, this moment!" cried Mrs. Paragreen; "let us shake off the dust of this place from our feet as quickly as possible."

"Farewell, sweet daughter of a cruel mother!" went on Mr. Shuffrey, following the fugitives to the door; "may your path in life be strewed with roses — may all happiness attend you. Such is the farewell hope of — Jerome. See to the door."

Here we would fain enter into a philosophical disquisition as to the causes of the unjust and unjustifiable prejudice which attaches to one of the most in earnest, and undoubtedly one of the most beneficial of the callings pursued by mankind. But this would take too long, and Mr. Paragreen is waiting for us, so we put off our lucubrations on the subject and hasten to rejoin our hero in his rambles.

CHAPTER XVI.

Catastrophe Number Two.

Though rather stunned by his own daring, and the unprecedented meekness of his wife after the offence he had given, Mr. Paragreen nevertheless recollected, while going down the stairs, that the Secretary had promised to call that morning at ten. Wishing to be polite, it occurred to our hero that he might as well call himself and ask after his new friend, and that, having Emma and Arabella with him, he could at the same time gratify the accomplished gentleman's wish to see them.

He therefore went and rapped at the Secretary's door, but in spite of the key being in the lock, no answer was returned. Mr. Paragreen, somewhat astonished, inquired on his way out, at the Bureau in the Court, if His Highness's Secretary was at home. The query occasioned a good deal of embarrassment among the few persons present, including the landlord, who stammered forth that His Highness and his Secretary had been summoned to St. Cloud. Mr. Paragreen expressed a hope that their absence would not be of long duration, to which the hotel-keeper replied, "He supposed not — probably but a few days."

"Bless my heart!" mused the little man, "it is very awkward. If we are not presented this week — and this is Tuesday already — God knows when we shall leave Paris, for, as to persuading Dora, especially in her present humour, to go home without having been to one of the Imperial receptions, I might as well try to persuade this Column to cross the Channel."

Mr. Paragreen and his three children were at that instant traversing the Place Vendôme, and the sight of the Column accounts for his forcible simile. The sun was very hot, Mr. Paragreen was in no walking mood, and the chesnut trees of the Tuileries held out a promise of shade and coolness. Mr. Paragreen accordingly led the way into the gardens, and having hired a chair, and a French paper, sat down to read the news.

His eyes were fixed on the words, but without taking in their sense; for his thoughts were busy with other matters. This was the tenth day of their sojourn in Paris, and each day represented a large outlay of ready cash—not an agreeable consideration in itself, and rendered still less so by the fact of the scanty return of comfort obtained for it: three stifling hot rooms up in a garret, when they had at their disposal a comfortable and well-sized villa, absence enhancing its size and airiness: tobacco-smelling cabs, and hackney coaches, not always to be had for any money, sweltering crowds, and cart-loads of suffocating dust, when there was in a tidy coach-house at home a spick-and-span clean phaeton, and a horse with a coat shining like satin, and a decent coachman, and quiet lanes with hedges of roses and honeysuckles to drive in, or a lovely garden, and thick shady shrubbery to walk in.

In short, Mr. Paragreen was home-sick, and would have sacrificed all the Highnesses and Courts and court-dresses in the world, to be once more safely housed in Eden Villa, Peckham. But there was no chance of this for Heaven knew how long. Would they had never met that Prince, who had brought them nothing, after all, but trouble! And to form the apex of his discomfort, there was the keen apprehension of what might be in store for him by two o'clock at the hotel.

"Let me see," speculated our little friend, "whether I can't find some way of making it up with Dora — some small present would do." This was a method that had answered well more than once, and one idea begetting another, the anxious husband came to remember a pair of ear-rings somewhere in the Rue de la Paix that Dora had much admired. "By jingo, I'll go and get them this instant — if they are not too dear."

Leaving Tobo, who was reading Galignani's Messenger, in charge of his sisters, hard at work skipping with some other English girls, with whom they had picked up an acquaintance, Mr. Paragreen went out of the gardens, and turned to the right into the arcade of the Rue Castiglione. As he walked along, his eye was caught by a display of curious coins in a money-changer's shop window, which unluckily suggested to him, that he might as well get some gold and silver for his paper money.

Mr. Paragreen, as a practical man, had always made a rule never to pay for small purchases with notes of comparatively large value — he contended that they excited the seller's greed; and on the contrary, that an offer in coin assured the buyer a good bargain. However this may be, Mr. Paragreen, on his road for the ear-rings, was reminded by the money-changer's shop window, that he was short of change — so in he went, and tendered the first note that came under his hand, (by chance the smaller one of the two he had received at Corazza's,) across the counter.

The money-changer examined the note, consulted a memorandum-book, and then saying with an unconcerned face, "Please to sit down, I bring you the money instantly," vanished into a back-room. Mr. Paragreen took a seat, and having nothing better to do, amused himself with watching the various individuals who stopped to look in at the window. Now it came to pass, that one of the faces, the scrutiny of which formed Mr. Paragreen's innocent pastime, bore such a likeness to that of the Marquis met at Corazza's, that Mr. Paragreen could have sworn it was the Marquis standing there before him, but for the complete absence of every trace of beard. However, he got up, and with no other intention than that of warning his noble acquaintance, if indeed it were he, of the mistake about the cards, he stepped nimbly forward, and touching the stranger's sleeve, said, "I beg your pardon, Sir."

The person so addressed turned, identified the speaker, and took to his heels. This action let in a sudden ray of light on the understanding of the confounded Paragreen; he received the instantaneous revelation that he had been duped, and forgetful of his 500 francs, and of everything but his revenge, the little man roaring out in English, "Stop thief! stop thief!" gave chase. The money-changer, who from the inner room had been keeping a vigilant watch, rushed out after his customer, shouting at the top of his voice, "Au voleur, au voleur!" The two sergens de ville sent for by the shopkeeper, arriving in the very nick of time, joined in the cry and in the race. Some of the idlers, and all the gamins in the street, followed to see the fun — and in less time than it takes to write it, poor hatless Mr. Paragreen was stopped, overtaken, seized by the collar, by the waistcoat, by the flaps of his coat, by every part, in short, of his garments, which afforded any hold to fifty grasping hands, and panting for breath, but protesting loudly he was "Anglais, Allié!" and that is was "l'autre," he was hurried to the nearest Commissaire de Police, the centre of a crowd of at least five hundred persons, the half of them sergens de ville, gendarmes, gardes de Paris, with a tambour major to boot.

The evidence of the money-changer was first taken, followed by that of the sergens de ville, who had effected the arrest; then addressing himself to the Englishman, the Commissary asked him his name, quality, and the object of his journey to Paris. (Useless to say that the Commissary spoke English, as every one did more or less during that time.) Mr. Paragreen gave his name, said he was a retired merchant, and that he had come to Paris to see the Exhibition. This answer made the Commissary look grim, as if he began to smell a rat. The fact was, that since the opening of the Palace of Industry, this French functionary had not had a moment's peace, having for the last three months done nothing but read, write, converse, think and dream of rogues of all sorts, of all nations, who had taken advantage of the Exhibition to make Paris their head-quarters. This had given him a sort of horror, not only of the great national undertaking, but of everybody, and everything connected with it.

"Where do you live?" inquired the Commissary.

"At the Hotel de l'Unicorne."

"Very good," said the questioner, smelling the rat more than ever. "Do you know anybody in Paris? Can you give any references?"

"I have the honour to be known to His Highness the Prince of — something, somewhere," replied Mr. Paragreen, drawing himself up haughtily.

"Better still — excellent," said the Commissary, rubbing his hands and hardly able to repress a laugh. "Please to explain how you obtained possession of — By the bye, have you any more billets de banque?"

"Yes, I have another," answered Mr. Paragreen, holding out the note for a thousand francs.

The functionary handed it to the money-changer, who after examining it, pronounced that it was one of the same stolen batch, and was stopped of course.

"Now, tell me how you came to be in possession of these two French notes."

Mr. Paragreen related at length how he had received them from a gentleman whom he had met at Corazza's Café.

"So that," resumed the magistrate, "when you presented this note to be changed you had not the least idea it was a stolen one?"

"Not the very least," affirmed Mr. Paragreen.

"What made you take to flight then?" said the Commissary.

"I did not take to flight. I saw the man who had cheated me looking in at the shop window, and I ran after him."

"You then knew that the notes had been stolen, since you say that the man had cheated you," urged the Commissary.

"I only guessed he had when I saw him take to his heels on confronting me," said Mr. Paragreen.

"According to your own account," pursued the functionary, "you exchanged bank-notes to the value of sixty pounds with an utter stranger, whose name you did not even know at the time — a very likely proceeding in a man of mature age, and who professes to have been a man of business. I would advise you to alter your system of defence, and tell the truth."

"There isn't a tittle to change in what I have told you," said Mr. Paragreen, stoutly. "If you don't believe me, send for my wife and children, they can swear to the truth of every word I have spoken."

"That will not do, my friend," said the Commissary, with a cunning shake of the head; "prudent rogues have been known before this to prepare and agree upon a story with their wives and children in the event of a mishap."

"Rogues may have done so. I am not acquainted with rogues' ways," retorted Mr. Paragreen scornfully.

"Once more," said the Commissary, sternly, "I warn you for your good against the course you are pursuing — you deceive nobody. Such extraordinary coincidences as you relate, the very man who gave you the notes looking in at the shop window where you are changing them, and so on — such things, I say, may be found in books, but not in real life. We see through it all. It was not a thief you were running after, but an accomplice — the look-out, who warned you of the approach of the sergens de ville. The trick is stale, and we are not Commissary of Police for nothing."

Mr. Paragreen rebutted the imputation with disdain.

"Sir," resumed the Magistrate slowly and impressively, for he was really a kind-hearted gentleman, "I am inclined to deal leniently with you, but you must help me. For the last time, I beg of you to renounce all subterfuge, and tell me plainly and truly how and from whom you got those banknotes."

Mr. Paragreen repeated angrily that he had already told the truth, and the whole truth.

"Very well, then, since you will have it so, take the consequences," said the Commissary; and turning to the police-officers present, "Au dépôt de la Préfecture de Police."

CHAPTER XVII.

Mrs. Paragreen to the Rescue.

MRS. PARAGREEN was practising how to walk in a manteau de cour, represented for the time being by a series of towels pinned together, and dragging on the ground behind her, when Tobo and his little sisters came in with the intelligence that their father had left them in the gardens of the Tuileries and never returned.

"Your father will break my heart some day," said Mrs. Paragreen, unpinning her train, "I know he will;" and she went straight to the faded yellow sofa, and sat down with the look of a judge, who only waits for the presence of the culprit to pass some awful sentence.

After a good half-hour of this suspense, a sound of knuckles against the door broke the silence. "Come in!" cried Mrs. Paragreen in her sharpest tones.

"Commissionaire!" said one of that body, opening the door.

"Begone!" shouted the lady on hearing the abominated name, "begone!"

"Une lettre pour Madame Barabry—"

Mrs. Paragreen got up, and no one can say to what extremities she might not have proceeded, had not her quick eyes discovered in time, that the address of the letter the Commissionaire held towards her, was in her husband's well-known writing. Making a snatch at it, she pushed the man out of the door with such a countenance as made him forget to ask for a pourboire, then breaking the seal with fingers that trembled, Mrs. Paragreen read as follows:—

"*Dépôt de la Préfecture de Police.*

"My dearest Dora,—Will you credit your own eyes, my dear, when you see that your unfortunate Sylvester is writing to you from a prison?"

"A prison!" gasped forth Mrs. Paragreen, "Sylvester in a prison! oh! the wretches!"

"Papa in prison!" chorused the children, and, with the exception of Tobo, they all began to cry.

"Hush!" thundered Mrs. Paragreen, "I won't have any blubbering, do you hear?" and she went on reading.

"Dépôt, they call it, the French for deposit — a very dirty one any way, and such faces round me! — to think that the father of a family — But to the point. The bank-notes were stolen after all, and are stopped, and that Marquis is a swindler. The Commissary would not listen to reason, and so here I am, God knows for how long, perhaps for ever, — if you don't manage to get me out — as I am sure you will, somehow or other. Only once make up your mind that out I must come, and out I shall come. But be quick about it, my dear — to-morrow will be too late; for if I am to spend the night in such company, I feel that I am *flambéd*, as that Count General said. So pray, make haste, if you wish, as I hope you do, to live the wife and not the widow of your miserable but loving husband,

SYLVESTER PARAGREEN.

"*P. S.* — By the by, I forgot — who do you think I found here? — why His Highness and his

Secretary — both victims they say, of Russian Machiavelism, which got at them even in Paris. I don't wonder at it, seeing that I myself — but I must stop — unless they are swindlers also, like that confounded Marquis, I mean the Corazza one, and not the other — God bless him for a true nobleman as he is! How could you mistake him for a — never mind — yours in haste. S. P.

"*P. S.* — The bearer is paid, remember."

Mrs. Paragreen, without uttering a single word, put on her Broad Brim, in the same silence tied on those of Emma and Arabella, motioned to Ida and Tobo to follow her, and went off like a shot to the British Embassy. "Qui demandez-vous?" asked the Concierge running after them.

"Sang Excellengs," said Mrs. Paragreen.

"Son Excellence est à Saint Cloud."

"BRICKS and MORTAR!" shouted the lady, fixing on the man's face a pair of eyes that might have intimidated three-headed Cerberus himself.

"Voyez plutôt à la Chancellerie," said the Concierge, with a politeness quite supernatural in so high a functionary, and pointing to a doorway on the right of the lodge. Mrs. Paragreen passed through it, threaded a dark passage, and as if thoroughly at home, turned the handle of the first door she came to.

"What do you want?" inquired in a rather gruff voice, and frowning at the intruder, a middle-aged gentleman, who, happening to be "dressed in a little brief authority" by the temporary absence of his superior, the Consul, was determined to make the most of it.

Mrs. Paragreen made her children come in one by one, then said, "What do I want? vastly polite of you to ask me in that way — I want back my husband, Sir."

"Your husband?" exclaimed the official.

"Yes, Sir, my husband, who has been cheated out of his money, and then put into prison by those blackguards of the French police."

"Madam, I beg of you to respect —"

"Fiddle, faddle — Jeuse take them! I want to have my husband back. I come here to have him back, and you must get him back for me, you must."

The official thus appealed to, perceived at a glance that playing the authoritative would not do with his present customer, and therefore begged Mrs. Paragreen to explain herself, which she did not over clearly, closing her tale by shewing the letter she had received from her husband.

The Consul's representative read the letter through, then observed with much gravity, "I am very sorry, Madam, but at this stage of the affair I do not feel justified in interfering."

"Don't feel justified in interfering!" repeated Mrs. Paragreen, with the burst of a bombshell, and sticking her arms a-kimbo. "Have you no husband — wife, I mean — no children, no feeling, no heart, that you tell me in that cool way, you don't feel justified in interfering? Does the country pay you to trim your nails, while English wives are robbed of their husbands?"

"Pray," said the gentleman, "don't be violent" —

"Don't be violent! I will be violent, Sir; I'll go into the street and make a row; I'll call upon all the English in Paris to come, and help me to burn down that vile dépôt of police, I will"—

The cataract stopped of its own accord. Mrs. Paragreen lifted up her right hand as if to entreat silence, that she might listen to voices on the other side of the partition. In another instant she had made her exit on tiptoe, gone to the door of the next room, flung it open, and made a rush at one of the two gentlemen there, crying out, "Here's the two-penny Marquis, who robbed my husband and sent him to prison; here's the swindler who stole the banknotes—I give him in charge.—Send for the police, I say."

"The woman is mad—I never saw her before in my life," cried the Corazza grandee, trying in vain to disengage himself from Mrs. Paragreen's iron grasp.

"Ah! you never saw me before, didn't you?—and you never saw these innocent creatures you have robbed of their father, eh!—speak out Ida, Tobo, Emma, and Arabella—did you ever see this fine gentleman before?"

Ida, Tobo, Emma, and Arabella shouted out that

the person was the one they had met at Corazza's, who called himself a Marquis, and with whom their father had exchanged some bank-notes.

"Do you hear them?" said Mrs. Paragreen, addressing herself to officials No. 1 and No. 2, (the one of the brief authority, and the other they had found conversing with the false Marquis;) "do you hear what these innocent creatures say, and can you doubt their veracity? Send for the police, I say — have him searched, and I'll be bound you'll find more of the stolen bank-notes somewhere about him."

Both officials looked very puzzled.

"To confound this fury," said the man, with a great show of offended dignity, "I have no objection to my pocket-book being examined — will you allow me to pull it out?"

"Certainly," said Mrs. Paragreen; "Tobo, and you Ida, stand at the door, I'll look after this open window myself."

As soon as he was released, the accused took out his pocket-book, but in doing so, something fell out of his pocket, and rolled on the ground; a something else, that in all likelihood he did not intend to show, as he made a dash to recover it. But Mrs. Paragreen was beforehand with him; quick as lightning she picked up a paper crushed and crumpled almost into a ball.

"There, take it," said she, handing it to official No. 1; "I'll lay you any wager it's some new proof of roguery."

Official No. 1, after unfolding and smoothing out the paper, looked at its contents, and exclaimed in surprise — "Why, it is an English passport that I signed myself not an hour ago!"

Official No. 2 examined the paper, and exclaimed in his turn — "Dear me! only five minutes ago it was here with these other passports — this person must be a conjurer, and conjured it off my table into his pocket."

"Not intentionally, I protest" —

"Reserve your explanations, if you have any, for another place," interrupted official No. 1, ringing the bell, "the theft is flagrant."

There was not much room for doubt, to be sure. The *soi-disant* Marquis having cogent reasons, as may be inferred, for desiring a creditable passport, had hit on a scheme to procure one that betrayed a certain fertility of invention, coupled with a thorough knowledge of the ways of the British Consulate. He called on the employé who has charge of and distributes the passports left to be viséd, and while parading a cane of Manattee hide, for which he wished the Ambassador's patronage, he pocketed a gentleman's passport, and would have succeeded in carrying it off but for our heroine's quick ears.

The servant who answered the bell was ordered to fetch a policeman immediately — an affair of five minutes, — and official No. 1, after giving the subtractor of passports in charge, left the office, probably to ask for instructions from some of his superiors, for he said, on returning to Mrs. Paragreen, "Now, Madam, if you please, I am ready to accompany you to the Préfecture of Police, to see what can be done to get Mr. Paragreen out of this scrape."

Mrs. Paragreen was naturally all impatience to be gone; accordingly, three coaches were sent for, in which all the actors in the preceding scene, official

No. 2 excepted, took their seats, — the swindler and police officers, of course, in one by themselves.

As they drove along, the Consul's representative begged Mrs. Paragreen to give him a detailed and more connected account of her husband's dealings with the pretended Marquis, in the course of which she naturally mentioned the visiting card and invitation to dinner, and the awkward situation in which they had found themselves with the real Marquis de la Motte d'Or. This circumstance struck the official as one that might be turned to use, and he remarked, that he had no doubt, if the attendance of the Marquis could be procured, Mr. Paragreen's character would be instantly cleared.

At Mrs. Paragreen's suggestion, Tobo was transferred to the first empty cab they met, and despatched to No. 43, Rue Las Cases, charged by his mother to do all he could to induce the Marquis to accompany him to the Préfecture — a most agreeable commission to Tobo, who felt that at last he was being treated as if he were a man.

The reader guesses the rest. The gentleman from the English Embassy had scarcely finished stating the case to the Prefect, and declaring his own strong conviction of Mr. Paragreen's innocence, when the Marquis de la Motte d'Or came in with Tobo, and confirmed the truth of Mrs. Paragreen's story, adding, that, as far as he could judge, Mr. Paragreen was the last man in the world to take anybody in. The Prefect immediately wrote an order for Mr. Paragreen's release, and courteously handing it to Mrs. Paragreen, desired some of the officers of the court to proceed to the dépôt with the lady; and in a very few minutes husband and wife were in each other's arms.

"There, old boy!" cried Dora, flourishing the Prefect's order.

"Hurrah!" shouted Sylvester, "I was sure you would get me out. Bless your brave heart!"

And then, for the first time since the sad intelligence of her husband's imprisonment, Mrs. Paragreen gave way, and began to cry like a very woman. "Never mind," sobbed she, "it is—for—joy!"

The parting with the Marquis took place amid a general discharge of tears and smiles, and never were warmer or sincerer thanks given than those offered to him by the Paragreen family.

"And now," said Mrs. Paragreen, as she was getting into a coach, "to the Hôtel to pack, and *en route.*"

"That is a blessed word," cried Mr. Paragreen, "*en route.* Hurrah for home!"

The first thing done on reaching the hôtel was to ask for the bill and settle it, then all, little ones included, set to work packing. While thus busied, what should arrive but the uniform and the manteau de cour! They were paid for, and packed with the rest, Mr. Paragreen observing, as he helped to push them into one of the trunks —

"After all, Dora, dear, uniforms, and manteaux, and drawing-rooms, and all that, I have no doubt, are very good things in their way, but *home*, and *comfort*, and LOVE, are better still."

"Why, Sylvester, if the truth must be told, the same thought came into my head when I saw you again, after the horrid fright I was in that I had lost you."

By the eight o'clock train of the same evening the Paragreen family left Paris, and on the morrow, at mid-day, were quietly installed at Eden Villa, Peckham, where we leave them, wishing them and the reader

A MERRY CHRISTMAS.

PRINTING OFFICE OF THE PUBLISHER.

www.ingramcontent.com/pod-product-compliance
Lightning Source LLC
Chambersburg PA
CBHW032141230426
43672CB00011B/2411